W9-BKK-792

THE
WORLD OF MUSIC

Rock and Roll:
1955-1970

THE

WORLD OF MUSIC

Rock and Roll:
1955-1970

RICHARD CARLIN

Facts On File Publications
New York, New York ● Oxford, England

THE WORLD OF MUSIC
Rock and Roll: 1955-1970

Copyright © 1988 by Richard Carlin

All rights reserved. No part of this book may
be reproduced or utilized in any form or by any
means, electronic or mechanical, or by any information
storage and retrieval systems, without permission
in writing from the publisher.

Library of Congress Cataloging-in-Publication Data

Carlin, Richard.
   Rock and roll, 1955-1970.

   (The World of music)
   Includes bibliographies and index.
1. Rock music—1951-1960—History and criticism—
Juvenile literature. 2. Rock music—1961-1970—History
and criticism—Juvenile literature. I. Title.
II. Series: World of music (New York, N.Y.)
ML3534.C32   1988   784.5′4′009045   87-36422
ISBN 0-8160-1383-7

British CIP data available on request

Printed in the United States of America

10 9 8 7 6 5 4 3 2 1

Contents

PREFACE   ix

1. THE ROOTS OF ROCK   1

The Folk Basis   1
Musical Instruments   2
From Swing to Jump   5
Birth of the Electric Blues   6
Stomping at the Honky Tonk: White Stars
    of the Postwar Years   9
Read   11
Listen   12

2. FROM RHYTHM
AND BLUES TO
ROCK AND ROLL   13

The Impact of Records and Radio   13
Doo Wop, Sh' Boom!   15
Solo Stars: Fats Domino and Chuck Berry   18
Rockabilly Stars   21
Read   23
Listen   24

3. LEGENDS: ELVIS, LITTLE RICHARD, AND BUDDY 25

Elvis, the King   26
Wop Bop Alu Bop a Wop Bam Boom!   30
Teen Idol from Texas: Buddy Holly   34
Read   35
Listen   36

4. TEEN IDOLS 37

The Brill Building: New York's
   Rock Factory   37
Lieber, Stoller, and Spector:
   The Wall of Sound   39
Manufactured Stars of the Early 60s   41
The Pick of the Crop: True Artists
   of the Early 60s   44
Read   48
Listen   48

5. MOTOWN AND SOUL 49

The Forebears   49
Motown   51
Soul   57
Read   60
Listen   60

6. THE BRITISH INVASION 63

The Beatles   63
The Rolling Stones: Bad Boys of
   Rock and Roll   70
Read   74
Listen   74

7. **THE TIMES THEY ARE A-CHANGIN': THE AMERICAN ROCK SCENE, 1964-69**   77

The Folk Revival   77
The San Francisco Sound   83
Read   88
Listen   89

8. **THE SUPER GROUPS**   91

The Kids Are Alright: The Who   91
Power Trio: Cream   95
The Doors   96
The Band   99
Read   102
Listen   102

9. **POSTSCRIPT: WOODSTOCK**   103

GLOSSARY   105

INDEX   111

Preface

Long hair. Love beads. Purple satin pants. Pompadours. Screaming electric guitars, smoke bombs, and thumping drums. Four mop-topped youths in collarless suits. Screaming girls fainting in the aisles. Three women in high heels and miniskirts singing "Where Did Our Love Go?"

A parent's nightmare? Symbols of our age? The culmination of American art?

All of these images come from the world of rock and roll, America's most explosive music. For teenagers everywhere, rock and roll has been a music of liberation, the expression of their frustrations and dreams. Yet, books about rock and roll written for teens tend to focus on personalities. Few have tried to relate rock and roll to the history of American folk, pop, and jazz, or traced its history in the golden years, 1955-1970.

This book treats rock and roll with the seriousness—and frivolity—that it deserves. It traces the history of rock from its roots in twentieth-century American pop music, and then gives a balanced portrait of the growth of rock through its many styles—rhythm and blues, teenie bop music, Motown and soul, British groups, the San Francisco Sound, and Woodstock. Focusing on the highlights, it is a selective history that is meant to serve as a starting point for further exploration.

Rock and roll is uniquely American. It grew out of the relation—sometimes good, sometimes bad—between America's two largest communities, black and white. From black America came the rhythm, from white America the musical form. For many years, black and white artists were segregated in our culture, either by choice or circumstance. Rock and roll is the unique tribute to the power of integration. Although blacks and whites were kept separate, a few pioneering musicians joined together in America's urban centers and throughout the rural South. For them, the barriers between race were artificial.

Chuck Berry, a black artist, performed at white dances throughout the South, and took a white song, "Ida Red," and molded it into one of the first hits of rock, "Maybelline." Elvis Presley, a white artist, emulated black bluesmen who performed in his hometown of Memphis. Elvis dared to be different; dressing, walking, and talking like a black man, he challenged the forces of racism with his every move. The success of Elvis paved the way for hundreds of lesser imitators but also helped open the door for black artists who otherwise would not have been welcome in mainstream America.

From black and white cultures came the musical seeds of rock. From black culture came the blues, an intensely personal music that expressed the loneliness and depression of many blacks who faced personal tragedy. From white culture came the up-tempo dance numbers, the happy-go-lucky songs of America on the move. Rock appeals to both strong emotions, to despair and elation.

Rock and roll is a unique mixture of the genuine and the artificial. Rock is music that is manufactured, like any other product, to be sold to us through record companies, radio stations, even movies. When a performer becomes a star, large companies profit from the sale of records, concert tickets, and sheet music. Attempts to create stars by analyzing the teen market are not uncommon, and some have been successful.

On the other hand, the true stars of rock have been born, not manufactured. No one could have had the foresight to manufacture the Beatles. They were four unique individuals who grew up in the poorer neighborhoods of the English seaside industrial town of Liverpool. No one could have created Little Richard; his flamboyant dress and wild performances could not have been crafted by even the most far-sighted record executive. No one could have predicted the success of Bob Dylan, an immensely talented writer who leaps effortlessly from folk to rock to country to gospel.

Rock and roll is dynamic. As I write these words, there are hundreds of new groups performing at thousands of clubs. I cannot tell you what the shape of rock will be in five years, or even one year. However, a knowledge of its history is important to rock, as with any type of music. Today, when there is a revival of interest in the 60s and a continuing nostalgia for the 50s, it is more interesting than ever to take a look backwards at the past stars of rock and roll. Perhaps in this history you can catch a glimpse of the next wave.

Richard Carlin

Also in this series:

Man's Earliest Music: An introduction to musical terms, music notation, and musical instruments, and a brief introduction to four musical cultures from around the world: the Pacific Islanders, the Australian Aboriginals, the African Pygmies, and the Native Americans.

British and American Folk Music: A history of these vital folk traditions, including dance music, ballads, lyric songs, musical instruments, Black American music, immigrant and ethnic music, modern country, and the folk revival.

European Classical Music, 1650-1800: An overview of the classical period in Europe, including terminology, an introduction to the instruments of the orchestra, vocal and instrumental forms, and the great composers, with special emphasis on the lives of Bach, Mozart, and Beethoven.

The Roots of Rock

THE FOLK BASIS

America's popular music, including rock and roll, is a product of the melding of black and white cultures that occurred on the American continent. In order to better understand rock, we need to take a brief look at the musical traditions of these two cultures.

Black folk music has its roots in African styles. It is highly rhythmic, often emphasizing the interplay between two or more rhythm parts. For example, a singer accompanying him- or herself on guitar might sing in one rhythm while playing a different one. *Call and response* is an integral part of the black folk style: A leader sings one line (the "call") and then the group "responds" by singing a refrain. Black vocal style is often raspy or throaty sounding, closer to shouting than singing. This is particularly true in songs expressing deep feeling, including gospel or religious songs. Song lyrics often consist of fragments or phrases, often unrelated, that are grouped together.

In white folk forms, the emphasis is on telling a story. Most white folk songs are composed in *stanzas*, usually four lines long, and the melody is composed to fit the lyrics exactly. The same melody will be repeated throughout a song as new stanzas are sung. A *chorus* may be inserted between stanzas for the group to sing together or as a way of holding together the story line. Rhythms tend to be fairly regular. Vocal styles run the gamut from very relaxed, open-throated singing to intense, closed-throated, powerful sounds.

Both whites and blacks share a dance-music tradition. The music of the country or string band provided entertainment for an evening's dance both in the plantation hall and in the slave quarters. The fiddle, from the white tradition, and the banjo, from the black, were the most common instruments heard at a country dance. The melodies were usually simple, with an emphasis on maintaining a regular beat. The most popular form was the "reel," a quick dance style in $\frac{4}{4}$ time.

These folk elements appear in the rock style. Early rock is a dance music, in $\frac{4}{4}$ time, that emphasizes a hard-driving rhythm over lyrics. The vocalist is often the "leader," calling out one line, which is then addressed by the backup singers. The vocal sound varies from mellow crooning (closer to traditional white vocal styles) to frenzied shouting (closer to traditional black vocal styles). Typically, rock songs are based on stanzas accompanied by a recurring melody (this is clearly from the white tradition). However, some rock songs are closer in style to a series of unrelated lyric fragments (recalling black traditions).

MUSICAL INSTRUMENTS

The Introduction of the Guitar

Towards the middle of the nineteenth century, a new instrument, the guitar, originally from Europe, appeared on the scene. Black musicians used the guitar as a second voice, to mimic the vocal line by picking individual melody lines on a single string. They also played *syncopated* rhythms, by picking a steady beat on the bass strings and then playing melody notes on the treble strings on the off-beats (or between the steady bass pulses). By bending a string (pushing against it with the fretting hand), the musician could create notes that fall in between the notes of the scale; these "blue notes" widened the melodic possibilities. These important guitar techniques would have an influence on rock and roll.

White guitarists used the I-IV-V$_7$ progression, a simple grouping of chords, that could accompany just about any folk or pop song. They used a pick to strum across the strings, establishing a regular beat. Some white guitarists also developed a technique of playing runs (or groups of notes) on the bass strings to serve as bridges between the chords. These bass runs became more complex as more musicians developed new "licks" or techniques for playing a series of notes.

The Electric Guitar

The electric guitar was developed for a single purpose: to make the guitar louder so it could be heard in a large jazz combo. The designers of the electric guitar could hardly have imagined that by simply adding a pickup and connecting a guitar to an amplifier they were creating an entirely new instrument. But this is exactly what happened.

The technique used in playing electric guitar is totally different from that used in playing an acoustic guitar. For one thing, the *sustain* of each note—or how long it will sound—is greatly enhanced. This means that after a note is struck, it will continue to be heard. A talented musician can alter the sound of the note by bending the string, or tapping on it, or by manipulating the pick in his hand—all as it continues to sound.

One thing guitarists discovered in the early days, when amplifiers were rather crude, was *distortion*. Quite simply, distortion of the sound (a fuzzy, grainy tone) happens when you turn up the amplifier too high, beyond the capabilities of the speakers. Another effect that can only be obtained on the electric guitar is *feedback*. It is created by the electrical interference between the pickup in the guitar and the amplifier. The result can be a high-pitched squeal. Although early electric guitarists probably discovered feedback by accident, later rock guitarists used it to add texture to their music.

Charley Christian (1916-1942) was the first important electric guitarist on the scene. Although he performed jazz, he came from a blues background, and his music showed a blues influence.

Charlie Christian. Courtesy Frank Driggs Collection

Christian's single-string guitar solos, in which he would push up against the strings with his fretting hand (called "bending the strings") to create half and quarter tones, had a great influence on the next generation of electric pickers. The bluesmen that followed were rougher than Christian, but they borrowed many of his techniques.

Another influential early electric guitarist was Aaron "T-Bone" Walker (1910-1975). Walker's advanced knowledge of chord harmonies led him to introduce 9th chords and other sounds often used in modern jazz. He also played rapid *arpeggios*, or chords broken into a series of notes played as runs. He is most famous for the song "Stormy Monday," which was a hit in the 1970s for the Allman Brothers, a highly influential Southern rock band.

Caressing the Keys: From Ragtime to Boogie Woogie

After the guitar, the second most important instrument in rock and roll is the piano. Some of the greatest figures in rock—from Little Richard and Jerry Lee Lewis to Elton John and Billy Joel—have made a rocking piano style the basis of their music.

Ragtime was the first truly American style of piano playing, originating in the Midwest at the end of the nineteenth century. Scott Joplin (1868-1917) is generally credited with popularizing this style with his "Maple Leaf Rag," published in 1899. This style introduced syncopation (or emphasizing the off-beats) to American music. Most rags are written in march time, or a slow, steady $\frac{4}{4}$. The left hand keeps a steady beat. On top of this rhythmic layer is placed the right hand, or melody, part. This part is syncopated; many of the melody notes fall in between the steady beat of the bass. This syncopation is achieved primarily by using dotted 8ths followed by 16ths.

Other piano styles were developing across the country during Joplin's lifetime. In New Orleans, Ferdinand "Jelly Roll" Morton (1885-1941) was creating a piano style that was more energetic and less pronouncedly "ragged" than Joplin's. Meanwhile, in the same year that the "Maple Leaf Rag" appeared, Baltimore-born composer Eubie Blake (1883-1985) published his "Charleston Rag," which features a "walking bass." In this style, the bass figures break away from the regular ragtime pattern to one in which individual notes move in dynamic patterns. This style paved the way for boogie woogie, a rollicking piano style based on the walking bass that became popular in the 1930s.

Along with boogie woogie, jazz styles were developing that emphasized the more lyrical, smooth aspect of the piano. These styles—most notably stride piano—were still syncopated, but the syncopation was more subtle. Whereas boogie was a purely instrumental style, stride stylists could accompany singers, using the piano part to mimic the human voice. The emphasis was less on the heavy, powerful bass runs of boogie to the more tender, lyrical melodic qualities that could be drawn from the piano.

Both boogie and stride were important elements in the evolution of the piano style that would be part of rock and roll. Rock borrowed the energy and rollicking bass of boogie, while drawing on some of the smoothness and lyricism of stride. The result was high-powered playing the likes of which had never been heard before.

FROM SWING TO JUMP

In the 1930s and 40s, several new styles of popular music developed in America's urban centers. One hotbed was St. Louis, where a new form of blues-influenced jazz was growing in the early 1930s. William "Count" Basie (1904-1984), a local piano player and bandleader, was most influential in transforming the blues into dance music, creating a new style called "swing."

Swing was much smoother than ragtime or early jazz, in order to accommodate the needs of dancers. Swing musicians performed in dance halls; while they might be admired as artists, they were expected to propel the dancers' feet by providing a regular, predictable beat. Swing was definitely syncopated, but the syncopation was better integrated and more thoroughly planned than in earlier forms of jazz.

Swing bands ranged in size from small combos to big bands. Although brass instruments often took the lead, swing combos also featured guitar, piano, and sometimes even violin.

Along with the development of swing came bigger bands playing for larger halls. Big bands meant big sound; part of the impact of the swing band was the sheer volume produced by so many pieces. In the days before widespread amplification, the big bands came closest to producing what a four-man heavy metal rock band can do today: create a total experience of pulsing music and dancing bodies. The steady beat literally made the skin jump, propelled by the power of the massive brass sections. Meanwhile, among urban black performers, swing progressed into jump, a more lighthearted but still highly rhythmic style. A master of this style was Louis Jordan (1908-1975), who sang comic and novelty songs.* His first hit came in 1942, and for the next ten years he continued to produce discs that found a wide audience among blacks and whites. The "shuffle rhythm" that Jordan employed—a swinging, syncopated use of dotted 8th notes followed by 16ths—was emulated by early rock artists such as the white Bill Haley (see below) and the black Chuck Berry (see Chapter 2).

BIRTH OF THE ELECTRIC BLUES

Chicago was one of the important capitals of what today is called electric or urban blues. Country blues singers were usually lone performers, typically a man with a guitar singing on street corners or at county fairs for handouts. In the cities, this style was modified and updated. The sad, howling vocal style was maintained, but it was set in an entirely new mode. The single guitar was replaced by a combo. The most important element here was the new lead instrument, the electric guitar. Drums, piano, and harmonica (called a "blues harp") were also part of this small, swinging band.

Muddy Waters: From Mississippi Delta Blues to Chicago Innovator

McKinley Morganfield (a.k.a. Muddy Waters; 1915-1983) was born and bred in the Mississippi Delta, an area of fertile countryside and hardworking farmers that was the spawning ground for many of this century's greatest blues musicians. His nickname, "Muddy Waters," represents everything that is best about Delta blues: the muddy, dark, foreboding quality of the music and lyrics; the depth and moving experience of the rushing Mississippi waters.

Muddy began his career as an acoustic guitarist influenced by other blues greats. He knew, and idolized, and for a time studied with the legendary blues guitarist Son House. Robert Johnson (c. 1912-

---

* Jordan's music has recently been revived by white "new wave" singer Joe Jackson. He has scored a hit with Jordan's famous novelty number "Is You Is or Is You Ain't My Baby?"

1937), who made a handful of 78 records in the late 1930s before being brutally murdered, was another early influence. Johnson's haunting blues sound, reflecting his own tormented life, has had an enormous impact on many of rock's great guitar players, including Eric Clapton and Duane Allman.

After struggling as a country blues artist and sharecropper, Muddy traveled to St. Louis and then to Chicago in search of better work. Driving a truck by day during his first two years in the Windy City, Muddy began appearing at local clubs. Over the next few years, Muddy recorded such classics as "Rollin' Stone" (the song that inspired a group of English musicians, ten years later, to take the name "The Rolling Stones"), "I'm Your Hoochie-Coochie Man," "Got My Mojo Working," and "Tiger in Your Tank." Muddy's backup ensemble was pared down to the basics—sometimes just guitar and bass, sometimes two guitars, drums, and harmonica (or "harp"). Muddy's vocal style was pure Delta blues; a forceful, nearly shouting delivery. His stage presence was also forceful, exuding a raw sexiness that many rock stars, from Elvis on, have emulated.

Howlin' Wolf

Chester Arthur Burnett (1910-1976) earned his nickname, "Howlin' Wolf," from the deep, moaning howl that is a trademark of his singing style. Born and bred in the farm country of eastern Mississippi, Wolf worked as a farm laborer by day until he was in his 40s. He was influenced by several important country blues guitarists: Charlie Patton (1887?-1934), a recording star of the 1920s that Wolf said taught him to play guitar; Robert Johnson; and the more modern-sounding Mississippi Sheiks, a group of musicians centering around the Chatman family. The Sheiks's repertoire ran more towards "party blues" about women, sex, and drinking than the darker blues of Robert Johnson.

Wolf had decided to quit farming when World War II broke out, and he was called into the service. On his return, he formed his first combo, working out of West Memphis, Arkansas, from 1947 to 1952. He made his first recordings, and was featured regularly on local radio. In 1951, his song "How Many More Tears" made the rhythm and blues (R&B) charts, leading to his move to Chicago, the blues capital, in 1952.

Wolf's popularity was based as much on his stage presence and physical appearance as on his music. He opened his act by crawling across the stage on all fours and savagely howling like a wild animal. Wolf's music is almost monotonous in its intensity. Melodically simple, the records consist of rhythmic interplay between the various instruments and Wolf's vocal part. His own rhythm was freer than many more modern musicians, reflecting the influence of his country-blues musical background. It is the intensity of his vocals that really makes his records standouts.

B. B. King

Riley B. King (1925-   ), better known today as B.B., is the most modern, forward-looking electric bluesman. He is also the youngest. He gained his considerable knowledge of music primarily from records. His first job was as a disc jockey in Memphis, where he took the nickname "Beale Street Blues Boy" (Beale Street was Memphis's center of bars and whorehouses, where music was made from dusk to dawn.) This nickname was later shortened to B.B.

Although B.B.'s repertoire is strictly blues, including his signature piece "Every Day I Have the Blues," his music shows the polish and pure technique of the jazz virtuosi of his youth. This is particularly apparent in his single-string solos. He rarely bends the strings to create blue notes; instead, he uses a quick, flawlessly executed vibrato to play quarter and half tones that fall in between the cracks of the Western scale. His tone is always clean, with perfect intonation and

B. B. King. Courtesy Sidney A. Seidenberg Inc.

attack. His singing style, while incorporating some of the shouting intensity of other bluesmen, is mellower, and he uses dramatic pauses, singing slightly off the beat, to give his music a more laid-back, "cool" feeling.

STOMPING AT THE HONKY TONK: WHITE STARS OF THE POSTWAR YEARS

"Honky tonk" music is a term used loosely to describe the white country styles of the postwar years. The seeds of this music were planted in the 1930s. Particularly influential was the "Yodelin' Breakman," Jimmie Rodgers (1897-1933). Born in Meridian, Mississippi, the heart of black blues country, the singer is remembered today for his recordings made from 1927 to his death. Rodgers's bluesy vocals combined the lonesome sound of country balladers with the black bluesmen's love of bended notes. His "blue yodel," a combination of Swiss yodelling with a plaintive crying quality, was copied by countless singers. His death by tuberculosis at an early age insured his fame for years to come; reissues of Rodgers's music still sell well today.

The other major influence on postwar country music was western swing. Western swing was a crazy-quilt combination of country songs, string band instrumentals, blues, and jazz. These bands featured syncopated fiddles, vamping pianos, electrified guitars and "lap steel" guitars, drums, and even a large brass section. The electrified "lap steel," a forerunner of today's pedal steel, gave western swing its unique sound. By sliding a bar across the strings of the lap-steel, players were able to create everything from crying sadness to a bubbly, happy sound, mimicing the range of sounds that can be produced by the human voice.

The most influential band in this style was Bob Wills's (1905-1975) Texas Playboys, featuring Wills on fiddle and the "Hillbilly Bing Crosby," Tommy Duncan, on vocals. Duncan's smooth vocals were clearly modeled on crooners like Crosby. The band's hits were drawn from all types of music, from country hoedown tunes like "Ida Red," that Wills learned as a young fiddler in Texas, to blues in-fluenced songs such as "Sitting on Top of the World" and

"Mississippi Delta Blues." All of the music was transformed into high-energy, smoothly executed music that was perfect for dancing.

Hank Williams

King Hiram "Hank" Williams (1923-1953) came from a country background—the tenant farms of Alabama. Like many other rural whites, he was exposed early on to the music of black bluesmen, and he particularly admired a local street singer who went by the name of "Teetot." Williams's "professional" career began at the age of 13, when he started to perform in honky tonks, schoolhouses, and with traveling tent shows.

During the war, Williams took a brief hiatus from performing to work in a shipyard, but was soon back on the road. His first break came in 1949, when he signed with a Nashville-based music publisher and began recording for MGM. His first hit, "Lovesick Blues," featured a yodelling-type vocal technique, in which Williams purposely broke his voice, moving rapidly from his normal vocal range to a falsetto. The bluesy sound, the yodel, the simple accompaniment hearkened back to Jimmie Rodgers, but the more jazzy overall style and emphasis on the dance beat looked ahead to country rock. Williams's light, smooth vocal style made him perfectly suited for everything from jaunty fast numbers to real tearjerkers.

Williams's tragic death of a heart attack insured him the same mythic status that Jimmie Rodgers enjoys today. But there is more to his appeal than the tragic circumstances of his life. Hank Williams was the first country singer to achieve real success in pop music circles. He paved the way for rockabilly (see Chapter 2), a combination of country sincerity with the rock and roll beat.

Early Rock: Bill Haley and the Comets

Coming solidly out of America's country tradition was Bill Haley (1925-1981). Hailing from the middle of Pennsylvania, his first musical idols were Jimmie Rodgers and Hank Williams, who had encouraged Haley to make music early in his career. In his late teens, Haley achieved some success with a country combo, and performed on popular country radio shows such as the WLS Barn Dance.

Williams urged him to visit New Orleans, where many black musicians were working. He also introduced Haley to recordings by

Bill Haley and the Comets.
Courtesy Frank Driggs Collection

the popular Louis Jordan (see above). On returning to Pennsylvania, Haley landed a job at a local radio station as both a disc jockey (DJ) and performer. Every day, his country show was preceded by an hour of rhythm and blues (R&B). In Haley's own words, he wondered: "Why shouldn't a country-and-western act sing rhythm and blues music? It was unheard of in those days [the early 50s]. I didn't see anything wrong in mixing things up. I liked to sing R&B tunes and I sang them."

Haley's recordings with his group, which he dubbed the Comets, were just on the edge of rock. They certainly showed a strong western swing influence, along with the obvious R&B roots. Haley's most famous song, "Rock Around the Clock," has a jazzy swing to it, and its guitar solo is derived from the swing-style guitar heard on Texas Playboys's records. Still, the use of the word "rock" and Haley's more teen-oriented lyrics certainly placed him on the edge of an important new sound.

READ

Bane, Michael, *Who's Who in Rock Music*. NY: Facts On File, 1981.

Belz, Carl, *The Story of Rock (2nd ed)*. NY: Harper and Row, 1985.

Clifford, Mike, *The Harmony Illustrated Encyclopedia of Rock*. (4th ed). NY: Crown, 1984.

Guralnick, Peter, *Feel Like Going Home*. NY: Random House, 1981.

————, *Lost Highway*. Boston: David R. Godine, 1979.

Heilbut, Tony, *The Gospel Sound: Good News and Bad Times*. NY: Simon and Schuster, 1971.

Pareles, Jon and Patty Romanowski, *The Rolling Stone Encyclopedia of Rock and Roll*. NY: Summit Books, 1983.

Sawyer, Charles, *The Arrival of B. B. King*. NY: Doubleday, 1980.

Shaw, Arnold, *Black Popular Music in America*. NY: Schirmer Books, 1986.

————, *Honkers and Shouters: The Golden Years of Rhythm and Blues*. NY: Collier Books, 1978.

Swenson, John, *Bill Haley: The Daddy of Rock 'n' Roll*. NY: Stein and Day, 1983.

Ward, Ed, et al., *The Rolling Stone History of Rock and Roll* (Revised edition). NY: Summit Books, 1986.

LISTEN

Haley, Bill and the Comets, *Rock Around the Clock*. Decca 8225.

Howlin Wolf, *London Sessions*. Chess 60008

————, *AKA Chester Burnett*. Chess 60016.

Jordan, Louis, *Best Of*. MCA MCL 1631.

King, B. B., *Best Of*. ABC 5026.

————, *Anthology*. ABC 5611.

Muddy Waters, *Chicago 5 Golden Years*. Chess 427005.

————, *Hard Again*. Blue Sky 34449.

————, *Fathers and Sons*. Chess 2 127.

2

From Rhythm and Blues to Rock and Roll

Rock and roll is an outgrowth of an earlier style, rhythm and blues (R&B). Both terms were created by record company executives and radio disc jockeys (DJs) to give a label to the new teen-oriented music that was being created by black and white musicians. Without records and radio, the impact of rock would have been greatly limited. In this chapter, we'll look at how this new music grew, focusing on the early vocal groups and then examining the lives and legends of three major early rock stars: Fats Domino, Chuck Berry, and Jerry Lee Lewis.

THE IMPACT OF RECORDS AND RADIO

In the years before World War II, records had been issued in several different lines: classical, mainstream pop, country, and "race," the last category consisting of recordings by black artists. In the years after the war, the term "race" was dropped for the less objectionable "rhythm and blues."* This grab-bag term was applied more or less indiscriminately to all black music.

R&B was more than just a label; it helped define a new musical style. Basically, there were two camps in the R&B category. One group focused on fast-paced, high-energy music. These vocalists were usually accompanied by the basic urban blues combo (guitar-bass-drums), usually with the addition of a saxophone or other brass instruments. The other group of R&B performers imitated the style of popular white artists such as Frank Sinatra. These "crooners" (smooth and sweet vocalists) specialized in moderate-tempo love songs.

Rhythm and blues *and* the rock and roll of the 1950s were in many ways similar. R&B music was driven by its beat, with lyrics often taking second place to the overall sound and drive of the music. Groups were basically small combos made up of guitar, piano, bass, and drums. The subject of the songs began to coalesce around the trials and tribulations of teenagers. Suddenly there was a music created not for a specific race but for a specific age group, that between the sometimes turbulent years of 12 and 17. Record company executives would discover that teenagers were a large and powerful group because they purchased more records than all other age groups combined!

One of the first people to realize that white teenagers were buying R&B records in large numbers was Cleveland-based DJ Alan Freed (1922-1965), who hosted a program called the "Record Rendezvous." He had been playing recordings by mainstream white artists such as Frank Sinatra and Patti Page for his teen audience. A local record dealer invited him to his shop to watch the white teenagers as they selected the music that *they* wanted to hear. Freed was surprised to see them purchasing R&B records almost exclusively. He convinced his manager to let him play this music, and renamed his show the "Moon Dog Rock 'n' Roll House Party." Freed, conscious of the racial barrier between whites and blacks, was not willing to advertise the music as R&B, for fear of losing his white audience.

---

* Gospel music, a third important black art form, would also be found in this part of the record catalog, or occasionally in a special religious series.

The term "rock and roll" is rooted in black tradition. But Freed's use of the word helped open the style to white acts as well as black. It was to lead to a new type of music that was defined by style and sound, rather than race. Freed sponsored stage shows for white audiences that featured black acts, helping to break down racial barriers and laying the seeds for the success of the white rock artists of the 50s and 60s. Sadly, Freed's career ended in scandal when he was accused of accepting record company money to feature certain records on his radio show.

The small transistor radio—inexpensive to purchase, battery-operated so that it was easily portable—was as important to the generation of the 50s and 60s as the Walkman and boombox have been to that of the 70s and 80s. It freed teenagers to hear their music whenever and wherever they wanted to. In the 30s and 40s, the radio was a large piece of furniture that sat in the living room. The family would sit together while they listened to their favorite dramatic or musical programs. The small transistor radio made it possible for teenagers to break away from the family. Now teenagers could choose to listen to programs geared specifically to their tastes, like the "Moondog" show; although Mom and Dad might disapprove, they couldn't control their children's listening habits as they had done in the past.

Radio did something else. It made stars out of the announcers as well as the musicians! Freed was only the first in a string of DJs who would bring rock music to America's teenage audience. Others developed their own unique personal style. "Wolfman Jack" (Bob Smith) was a popular DJ in the Midwest who spoke in a gravelly, sinister voice; Murray the K (Murray Kaufman) was the most famous Easterner, whose fast-paced patter set the style for later DJs such as Cousin Brucey (Bruce Morrow).

DOO WOP, SH' BOOM!

As more blacks settled in urban centers, the street corner became an important place to "hang out." Particularly for teenagers, the street corner was the center of social life, whether bragging to friends, picking up girls or guys, or simply passing the time. Often, groups of friends would gather for another activity: singing. Street-corner groups didn't need to invest in musical instruments: they could create their own bands vocally, by imitating the sounds of the various instruments in the vocal parts. While one singer carried the melody, the rest would fill in with nonsense syllables: "doo wop, doo wop," "sha-na-na," "eh-toom-ah-ta," "dum-bee-oo-bee," and others that defy written expression.

The *doo wop* groups, as they came to be known, had two successful models: the jazzy Mills Brothers, who enjoyed 50 years of popularity, and the more suave Ink Spots. Both groups scored their biggest hits in the 1940s and early 1950s. The Mills Brothers were a harmony group, featuring innovative, jazz-influenced arrangements in which the vocal parts often imitated the sound of horns. The Ink Spots had a distinctive style based on one voice singing the words in a high tenor, often switching to falsetto, while a second voice recited the words in a deep baritone. These two ends of the spectrum—high-tenor and deep bass—would define the doo wop range.

Doo wop took its inspiration from the sound and style of R&B. The songs focused on the problems faced by most teenagers: loneliness, unrequited love, and loss of a boy- or girlfriend. Doo wop music featured a regular rhythmic pulse and, of course, the characteristic nonsense syllable refrains and fills* behind the vocal line. Once the doo wop style took hold in the early 50s, a seemingly endless stream of groups—like the Orioles, Moonglows, Dominoes, Robins, Platters, and Coasters—produced records to meet the rage for the music in the early and mid-50s. A phenomenon of this type of music were groups that became known as "one-hit wonders"; they would produce one very successful record and then disappear, never to be heard from again.

The Orioles centered around a group of Baltimore high-school friends who practiced singing in the stairwell of the Pennsylvania railway station, where their voices would echo off the damp walls. They came to New York in the late 1940s, scoring their first hit with "It's Too Soon to Know." Their best-known song was 1953's "Crying in the Chapel." Both songs express typical teen concerns: one, the anxious lover ("Too Soon"); the other, the abandoned loved one ("Crying").

The Drifters were a highly successful group, extending the popularity of doo wop well into the 1960s. The group was originally

---

* "Fills" are vocal parts used to "fill up" the gaps in the lyrics of a song, or to serve as a bridge from one part of a song to another.

The Drifters.
Courtesy Atlantic Records

created to back up lead vocalist Clyde McPhatter (1933-1972), whose smooth singing style had made the earlier group the Dominoes an enormous success. The Drifters's hits included "Save the Last Dance for Me" (1960), set at a high-school prom, and "Up on the Roof" (1962), a story of a teenager who escapes the everyday world by taking refuge on the roof of an apartment building.

The Coasters introduced comedy into the doo wop style. Their classic "Charlie Brown (He's a Clown)" and "Yaketty Yak" featured innovative vocal arrangements, using the bass voice to provide a comic counterpoint to the vocal. The famous refrain "Why's everybody always picking on me?" from "Charlie Brown," sung by the bass vocalist, could be every teenager's complaint. "Yaketty Yak" gives a teen's-eye view of the world of parents, and the many demands parents make on their kids.

The Coasters. Courtesy Atlantic Records

The Platters are perhaps the longest-lasting doo wop group. They are best known for two hits from the mid-1950s, "Only You" and "The Great Pretender."

SOLO STARS: FATS DOMINO AND CHUCK BERRY

The 50s saw the emergence of several important black performers in the rock and roll style. Although they were classified as rhythm and blues artists (because of their skin color), they were collectively creators of the rock and roll format, along with several key white counterparts.

The Fat Man

Antoine "Fats" Domino (1928-   ) came out of the boogie-woogie piano traditions of his hometown of New Orleans. His career, beginning in the early 1950s, is now well into its 30th year. The continued popularity of Fats Domino rests in his relaxed, pop-influenced vocal style, his driving piano playing, and his choice of material that ranges from country standards ("Blueberry Hill"), to jazz hits ("My Blue Heaven"), as well as more typical R&B-type material ("Ain't It a Shame," "I'm Walking").

Domino was born to be a musician. His father was a violinist who had performed with many New Orleans jazz bands, and his brother-in-law was a noted local pianist. At age 9, Fats began playing the piano, coached by his brother-in-law who marked certain boogie progressions on the keyboard for the young pianist to follow. By 14, he had found his true avocation, music, and he dropped out of school. At age 21, he met Dave Bartholomew, a trumpeter at a local club, who was the arranger and bandleader for all of his major hits.

While Domino's first single, "The Fat Man," was cast in the 12-bar blues form, its sound was entirely new. Rather than the angry or anxious sound of a blues shouter, Domino's vocal was subdued. The band was more rhythmically assured than most blues outfits, with an emphasis on the regular beat. Fats used triplets, played by his right hand, to embellish the basic melody. But overall it was the vocal effect that stood out on this and Fats's later hits. As Bartholomew put it: "We all thought of him as a country-and-western singer. Not real downhearted, but he always had that flavor, not the gutbucket sound." In other words, Fats was not a blues shouter, nor was he entirely a sad, tearful-sounding country crooner. Instead, his vocal style was upbeat and happy, with a smoothness borrowed from other pop singers.

Fats's success continued more or less unabated through 1963, with records consistently selling to audiences black and white. The "English invasion" of the 60s (see Chapter 6), along with Fats's leaving his original record label for a more lucrative contract elsewhere, led to a decline in his music. In 1968, he scored a hit with the Beatles's "Lady Madonna," and recorded a well-received comeback LP. Since then, he has continued to be a compelling live performer, enjoying success in clubs and concert halls, as well as in "50s revues" (groups of 50s artists touring together to play large halls as a "package show"), but has not been as active a recording artist.

The Duck Walk

One man in the 1950s nearly single-handedly created what would become known as "teen music," rock and roll songs with a jaunty beat, amusing lyrics, and a general good-time, party atmosphere created by vocalist and backup band. This man was Charles Edward Anderson—Chuck Berry (1926-   ).

Chuck Berry is best remembered today for a string of hits—his first big hit, "Maybelline," followed by "Rock and Roll Music," "Roll Over Beethoven," "Sweet Little Sixteen" and the semi-autobiographical rock anthem, "Johnny B. Goode" (with the memorable chorus, "Go——go Johnny, go—   Go——go Johnny, go").

Born in California, Berry was raised in a rural Missouri town near St. Louis. Like many other rural children, he sang in the church choir. His early musical influences came through the family radio and the phonograph. He heard the white country stars of the "Grand Ole Opry" (a radio show based in Nashville), the black country bluesmen, and the swinging jump music of Louis Jordan (see Chapter 1). All of these influences were melded together in Berry's music.

By the early 1950s, Berry, who worked as a hairdresser during the day, had a small combo in which he performed urban blues and comic

Chuck Berry. Courtesy Frank Driggs Collection

novelty numbers at night. Along with his pianist, Jimmie Johnson, Berry recorded two numbers, a blues song called "Wee Wee Hours" and a country song called "Ida Red." The two men took this record to Chicago, where bluesman Muddy Waters (see Chapter 1) steered them to his record label, Chess records.

The owner of Chess was mildly impressed with the blues number, but really loved the swinging version of "Ida Red." The only problem was that "Ida Red" was a song associated with white country singers, and Chess records owner Leonard Chess knew that a black audience would never buy it. So, he instructed Berry to rework the song, and the new version, renamed "Maybelline," became an instant hit.

"Maybelline" combines the best of white pop music with the new sound of black rock and roll. Berry's guitar playing is based on country riffs, but also incorporates the sounds of 40s jazz stars. The hard-driving combo that accompanies him keeps the energy level high, and the overall feeling of the song is one of good-natured fun.

Although Berry continued to show a mastery of different styles of music, feeling equally at home with blues, novelty numbers, and swing, as well as rock and roll, he is remembered best for those songs that fit solidly in the rock idiom. In songs like "Sweet Little Sixteen" and "Johnny B. Goode," he expressed a teenager's sense of rebellion, while the energetic sound of his music made it perfect for the local "sock hop" dance.

ROCKABILLY STARS

Rockabilly is a type of music that combines the energy of rock with the sound of country (or hillbilly) music. The early stars of rockabilly—Eddie Cochran, Johnny and Billy Burnette, Gene Vincent—created a sound defined by a booming guitar, slapped bass, and a regular beat. The rockabilly vocalists loved echo, an artificial addition made in the recording studio that made their voices stand out in front of the backup group. It was "blues with a country beat," in the words of Carl Perkins. The style would create many important stars: Jerry Lee Lewis, Carl Perkins, and the young Elvis Presley in the mid-50s; and Buddy Holly (see Chapter 3) in the later years of the decade.*

---

* The group The Stray Cats mimics the rockabilly sound, as do English singers Nick Lowe and, in some of his music, Elvis Costello.

Rockabilly was rebellious music; it was music created by "cats," as the musicians called themselves. Like the beatniks of the late 50s, the rockabilly stars created their own special culture, with its own language, dress code (leather and long hair combed up at a rakish angle), and style. Rockabilly was a young, country-based teenagers' rebellion against the stifling atmosphere of the South.

One of rockabilly's talented pioneers was Carl Perkins (1930-), the son of a Tennessee farmer. Perkins is best remembered for his rockabilly anthem, "Blue Suede Shoes," which was later covered by Elvis Presley and the Beatles. The song was supposedly composed in the middle of the night, when Perkins awoke with a sudden inspiration. He wrote the words down on a potato sack; his family was living in a housing project, and, in Perkins's words, "we didn't have reason to have writing paper around."

Although Perkins was influential, one rockabilly performer stood out above all the rest. He stretched the form to its limits, and his outrageous performing style lay the groundwork for later rock performers. His name was Jerry Lee Lewis, a.k.a. "The Killer."

The Killer

Jerry Lee Lewis (1935-) was raised in the tiny town of Ferriday, Louisiana; the nearest "big city" was Natchez, Mississippi. He began performing on the piano from the age of 15, playing in the popular boogie and western swing styles that were in demand in local bars and clubs. At the age of 21, he emigrated to Memphis, lured by the city's rich musical community.

There, he met Sam Phillips (see Chapter 3), the legendary head of a tiny recording studio. Phillips instructed him to "learn some rock and roll." Lewis produced a string of classic singles for Phillips. His first hit, "Whole Lot of Shakin'," defined his style from the opening chords, which were mercilessly pounded from the keyboard. The lyrics are vaguely suggestive, and in his delivery Lewis makes the most of every nuance. The song was a hit on the country, R&B, and pop charts, an almost unheard of achievement in the 1950s.

"Great Balls of Fire" was Lewis's other wonderful achievement. The frantic vocal, half-shouted, half-sung, has a maniacal energy, while the melodic riffs on the piano are played with near abandon. This raw energy that is just barely under control became a trademark of Lewis's style.

Lewis had his greatest impact as a performer on the piano. He was the first in a long string of flamboyant pianists in the rock field,

Jerry Lee Lewis.
Courtesy Frank Driggs
Collection

culminating in Elton John. Lewis would lift his leg up and run his foot across the keys, jump up on the piano stool, twirl around and dance, climb on top of the piano—anything to impress his audience and express his energy. These stage antics did not mask his incredible ability; if anything, he seemed to need to jump around to be able to play better. What mattered was not so much the music he was playing or the words he was singing, but *how* the music was played and the words were sung. Lewis was one of the first rock stars to make the performance an integral part of the song.

Lewis's career stopped abruptly in 1958, when his marriage to his 14-year-old cousin led fans and press to turn their back on him. Apparently, he had broken one tabu that even teenagers could not accept. Lewis continued to perform and record sporadically through the following years, although he never achieved the level of fame that he had in those few short years in the mid-50s.

READ

Bane, Michael, *White Boy Singin' the Blues*. NY: Penguin, 1981.
Berry, Chuck, *Chuck Berry*. NY: Harmony Books, 1988.

Fleece, Krista, *Chuck Berry: Mr. Rock 'n' Roll*. NY: Proteus Publications, 1983.

Groia, Philip, *They All Sang on the Corner*. Branchport, NY: Edmond Publishing, 1983.

Karsh, Edward, *Where Are You Now, Bo Diddley?* NY: Doubleday, 1986.

Lewis, Myra, and Murray Silver, *Great Balls of Fire*. NY: Morrow, 1982.

Millar, Bill, *The Drifters*. NY: Macmillan, 1981.

Palmer, Robert, *Jerry Lee Lewis Rocks*. NY: Delilah, 1981.

Tosches, Nick, *Unsung Heroes of Rock 'n' Roll*. NY: Scribners, 1984.

LISTEN

Berry, Chuck, *Greatest Hits*. Chess 321.

Coasters, *Greatest Recordings*. Atco 33171.

Domino, Fats, *30 Hits*. United Artists 104.

Drifters, *Save the Last Dance for Me*. Atlantic 8059.

Lewis, Jerry Lee, *Roll Over Beethoven*. Pickwick 6110.

Perkins, Carl, *Blue Suede Shoes*. Sun 112.

Platters, *Super Hits*. Pickwick 3236.

3

Legends: Elvis, Little Richard, and Buddy

Rock music is more than just lyrics and melody. It has two other key ingredients: sound and style. Its substance goes beyond what is put on record to what the audience sees and hears. The rock "sound" is something more than just the individual components—vocal, instruments, words, riffs, beat—that go into each record. And the style in which this music is performed is different than in any other type of music. The performers who molded this style and sound made a lasting impression on all rock music that was to follow.

There are many stars who emerged in the early years of rock, who had hit records and were popular touring artists. Then there were the legends, who shaped the history of rock and roll through their work. Legends are performers who have a mystique that is greater than their music, who change the way people walk, talk, dress, communicate, and, of course, sing and play music. The three artists in this chapter—Elvis Presley, Little Richard (Richard Penniman), and Buddy Holly—created a new type of music. These artists created new "sounds," and they performed this new music in a way that had never been seen before.

ELVIS, THE KING

Most important to the history of rock was a poor, white Southern teenager named Elvis Aaron Presley (1935-1977); his recordings and his concert performances changed the way rock music was made and played. It is not an exaggeration to say that without Elvis, there would have been no rock and roll explosion in the 60s and 70s.

Elvis was born on January 8, 1935, in Tupelo, Mississippi. His father was an unskilled laborer, working most of his life behind the wheel of a truck; his mother was a devoted housewife. Elvis was an only child; his identical twin brother died at birth, and his mother lavished attention on her only son.

Elvis's first exposure to music was through the church. In his description of a typical church service, Elvis explains the major influences on his rock music. They are primarily the sound and style of black music, and the energetic "performance" of the preacher:

> Since I was two years old all I knew was gospel music. We borrowed the style of our psalm singing from the early Negroes. . . . The preachers cut up all over the place, jumping on the piano, moving every which way. The audience liked them. I guess I learned from them. I loved the music. It became such a part of my life it was as natural as dancing, a way to escape from the problems and my way of release.

At age 10, Elvis won a local singing contest, which encouraged his parents to buy him a guitar for his 11th birthday. Elvis and his guitar were inseparable. When he was in high school, he would sit in the back of the classroom and strum away. At age 13, his parents relocated to Memphis, in the hopes of finding life easier in the city. In Memphis, Elvis was explosed to many of the leading black artists of the day, including B. B. King, Howlin' Wolf (see Chapter 1), and Sonny Boy Williamson.

In the urban atmosphere of Memphis whites and blacks could mix more easily than in a rural setting. White teenagers picked up black expressions, calling each other "cats"; young boys grew their hair long, sported sideburns, and dressed in brighter colors. Elvis loved black music and culture, and soon began wearing his hair flipped up in back (a style called a "duck tail"). He dressed more flamboyantly than other white teenagers dared to do, sporting pink or yellow shirts and white shoes. Although he dressed loudly, Elvis's personality was quiet; he was withdrawn, a loner who few others understood. After high school, Elvis took up truck driving like his father did before him, seemingly on the road to a life of hard work and low pay.

Memphis, as a center of musical activity, had its share of small clubs, radio stations, and small recording studios. One studio was operated by Sam Phillips (1923-   ), a talented recording engineer who early on recognized the popularity of black artists among white teenagers. Phillips began recording local black musicians, and selling these tapes to small record labels that specialized in marketing to black audiences. Phillips had a bigger dream, however: to sell his records to a white audience, a potentially bigger and wealthier market than could be found among blacks. In 1952, he formed his own label, Sun Records. His secretary recalls him saying: "If I could find a white man who had the Negro sound and the Negro feel, I could make a million dollars." This dream would come true with Elvis.

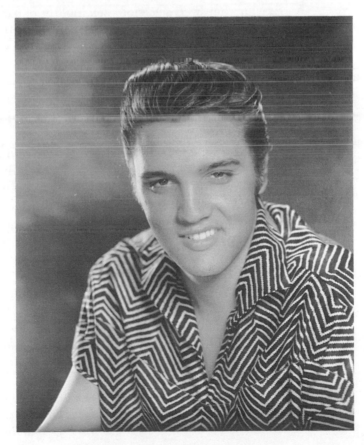

Elvis Presley. Courtesy RCA Records

Sun Records was not a very profitable business at first. In order to support himself, Phillips made his studio available to local musicians who wanted to record single records to give away to family or friends. Elvis came to Phillips to record a birthday record for his mother; perhaps he secretly hoped that the important record producer would recognize his talent. Phillips was not greatly impressed, but he did take a phone number where Elvis could be reached. Meanwhile, two other local musicians, guitarist Scotty Moore and bass player Bill Black, began hanging out in Phillips's studio. It was Phillips's idea to group the three musicians in order to create a "black" sound for the white vocalist.

The story of Elvis's first hit record, "That's All Right," released in 1954, is shrouded in myth. According to Scotty Moore, it was created during a break in recording when Elvis started to horse around by performing this old blues song, originated by black artist Big Boy (Arthur) Crudup. Sam Phillips contradicts Moore's account, saying that Elvis's version took months of hard work to create. In any case, the song is a classic in rock and roll history. It is one of the first records to be defined by its sound, more than its content. The song itself was hardly a classic, just a typical blues with some tried-and-true lyrics. But the sound—one of free-spirited abandon in the vocal and Scotty Moore's guitar licks—had never been heard before. In his vocal, Elvis expressed an attitude of cool defiance in a relaxed but powerful delivery.

Besides the sound of his music, Elvis's style was what really set him apart. In his early performances, he literally was all over the stage, crawling on all fours, taking leaps, and dropping to his knees, or doing splits. In a few years, he had refined his act, inspired mostly by film actors such as Marlon Brando (who appeared as a teenage hood wearing a leather jacket in the film "The Wild Ones") and James Dean (the most famous teenager of the 50s, who played a troubled youth in the film "Rebel Without a Cause" that Elvis is said to have viewed dozens of times). Elvis took a cool defiant attitude as he came up to the mike. He would sneer at the crowd, as if he didn't care how they reacted to him or his music. Then, he would slowly grind his hips, as if he were seducing his guitar. Before he even began to sing, the crowd had gone wild.*

---

* Ed Sullivan, the famous TV variety show producer, would not permit his cameramen to film Elvis's famous gyrating hips. Instead, when Elvis first appeared on the *Ed Sullivan Show* he was filmed only from the waist up.

Elvis Presley in concert.
Courtesy Frank Driggs Collection

Sam Phillips guided Elvis's recording career for two years after the release of "That's All Right," refining the special sound that he had created. An important figure came into Elvis's life in 1955 who was to replaced Phillips as the guiding light in his career. This was Colonel Tom Parker, a booking agent for concerts throughout the South who had previously represented country artist Hank Snow. Elvis became Parker's favorite and only client, and the Colonel dedicated himself to furthering the young man's career. As he himself put it, "When I first knew Elvis, he had a million dollars' worth of talent. Now he has a million dollars." Actually, the Colonel made many millions of dollars for Elvis.

Parker negotiated a record deal for Elvis with RCA in 1956. Initially, the company did well by the artist, producing a string of classics, including "Heartbreak Hotel," "Hound Dog," "Don't Be Cruel," and "All Shook Up." Although the big label added more elaborate backup vocals and instrumentation, it was Elvis's vocals that made these records such big hits. It was his combination of anger and energy that made these vocals so powerful. Elvis could make nonsense phrases like "Well-Uh-huh" sound as meaningful and expressive as polished lyrics. RCA also began giving Elvis slow love songs to record, including "Love Me Tender," in order to broaden his appeal to teenage girls who might be put off by *too* much sexual energy.

Although Elvis lived until 1977, his career effectively ended when he entered the Army in 1959. After his military service, he spent a good deal of time in Hollywood, churning out B-grade motion pictures. His later recordings lacked the power or creativity of his early work. Although he made a series of comebacks, beginning with a dramatic TV appearance in 1968 when he performed true rock and roll for the first time in nearly a decade, Elvis's last years were a sad parody of his earlier life. He grew bloated, performed in outlandish costumes, and was dependent on drugs. He became a prisoner of his own wealth, living in seclusion on his Memphis estate, Graceland (named for his mother). He died of an overdose of drugs.

Despite this unhappy ending, Elvis's legacy lives on in the recordings that he made in the mid-1950s. Countless artists have recognized his unique contribution, from the late 50s star Buddy Holly (see below), to John Lennon, who said that the Beatles's only ambition was "to be bigger than Elvis because Elvis was the thing."

WOP BOP ALU BOP A WOP BAM BOOM!

One artist who really put image and sound before lyric and melody was Little Richard (born Richard Penniman [1935-   ]). The same age as Elvis, Richard's career was also at its height in the mid-50s, although he continues to perform sporadically and is active as an actor and preacher today. Richard's impact was the result of his outlandishness: His lyrics were outrageously silly; his musical accompaniment was brazenly energetic; his use of makeup and his enormously high pompadour were shocking at the time; his style of dress took bright and bold to the limits of taste. Without Little Richard, artists as varied as James Brown, Alice Cooper, Kiss, Prince, and Michael Jackson could never have been accepted.

Little Richard's life story begins in Macon, Georgia, where he was born in a family of 12 children. Just as Elvis was raised singing in the church, so Richard's first musical experiences were with gospel music. He learned to play hymns on the piano. Many of his relatives were preachers, and his father and mother had little tolerance for authentic black music other than what was heard at church. Richard relates that the most popular music in his household was Bing Crosby, and the only black artist he heard while growing up was Ella Fitzgerald. As he later put it: "I knew there was something that could be louder than that, but I didn't know where to find it. And I found it was me."

Richard's father had little sympathy for his son's flamboyant character, which began to manifest itself in his early teen years. Richard left home at 13 and was raised by a white family that operated a local Macon nightclub. Three years later, Richard won a talent contest in Atlanta and was signed by RCA records. The recordings he made between the ages of 16 and 19, for a number of labels, were mostly of jump jazz songs or standard urban blues (see Chapter 1). Although Richard's characteristic wavering voice was present, the performances were not terribly interesting or original. He had yet to find his sound.

In 1955, Richard was back in Macon, working as a dishwasher in the local Greyhound station. He had sent a demo tape of his singing to Art Rupe, a producer/owner of a small Los Angeles-based label called Specialty Records. Rupe recognized Richard's potential and lined up seasoned musicians and a famous R&B studio in New Orleans for Richard's first Specialty sessions.

Little Richard. Courtesy
Frank Driggs Collection

Richard's first hit song came about through an accident. During the New Orleans sessions, he recorded a number of standard blues, again without really producing anything new. Then, as a joke, he ripped into a sexually explicit song that he had made up to amuse himself during breaks in his performances. Rupe recognized the brilliance of the song but realized that the lyrics needed changing. The cleaned-up version was released as "Tutti Fruiti," with the un-likely chorus: "A wop bop alu bop a wop bam boom!" It was an im-mediate sensation, selling more than 500,000 copies.

The lyrics to "Tutti Fruiti" are hardly inspired; they consist mostly of gibberish and humorous sexual innuendo: "Got a girl, named Daisy, she almost drives me crazy . . ." It's Richard's manic delivery, back by the high-powered band, that makes the song such energetic good fun. Here Richard introduced his signature wailing scream, "Wooooo," that the Beatles later imitated on a cover of Richard's own "Long Tall Sally."

Richard's vocal performance was matched by his stage presence. Examples of his manic energy, outrageous costumes, and use of eyeliner and lipstick are evident in three mid-50s movies, "Don't Knock the Rock," "The Girl Can't Help It," and "Mister Rock and Roll." In all, Richard turned out about 36 songs for Specialty, in-cluding the classic "Slippin' and Slidin'," "Long Tall Sally," "Good Golly, Miss Molly," and "Ready Teddy."

In gospel music, depth of feeling and belief is communicated through a shouted, ecstatic vocal sound. Richard drew on this gospel tradition, but used it to communicate what were essentially little pieces of nonsense. However, he sang with such energy and convic-tion that he was able to give nonsense a kind of sense of its own. Richard's melding of gospel with pop led the way for all "soul" singers that followed, from the frenetic James Brown to the more gospel-influenced Aretha Franklin, to the mellow sounds of Otis Redding.

Richard retired from rock in 1957, after his first conversion to evangelism. As an evangelical preacher, Richard turned his back on the "devil's music," and churned out a series of singles with no con-nection to the sound that he had worked so hard to create. Suddenly, we hear a subdued voice, although occasionally raised to the level of a preacher calling on his congregation to come back to God. Richard's first conversion lasted until 1964, when a new force entered the music scene: the Beatles (see Chapter 6).

When Richard realized that the Beatles were covering, successfully, his old songs and lifting many of his vocal techniques, he was eager to cash in on their success. For a period of about 14 years, he tried unsuccessfully to make a successful comeback, producing material that ranged from rehashes of his 1950s hits to records in the late 1960s and early 1970s that drew on the psychedelic sounds of Jimi Hendrix (who had earlier played guitar in one of Richard's touring bands).

Richard's stage appearance became even more outrageous as he sought, vainly, to recapture his audience. His costumes went from garish to worse, and he became somewhat of a joke in the entertainment industry. In 1978, he went through a second conversion, and since then has been active as a preacher. Recently, he made an appearance in the film "Down and Out in Beverly Hills," and may seek to start a new career as an actor.

In interviews, Richard rightfully shows pride in his considerable talents and achievements, but his claims to have "discovered" the Beatles and Jimi Hendrix should be taken with a grain of salt. His claims that his compositions were stolen from him by unscrupulous music publishers, unfortunately, are true. It is a sad repetition of what has happened many times in the music business, and not just to black performers. Young rock musicians, eager to be recorded, often sign away rights to their work, an action that they later regret.* But Richard's real achievement is not in either his boasting or his litigation to gain greater rights for composers. It is in his music and performances. In sound and in style, Richard laid the groundwork for such diverse groups as the Beatles and Prince and the Revolution.

---

* John Fogerty prefers not to perform any of his songs written when he was lead singer with Creedence Clearwater Revival because he does not receive royalties for them. Bruce Springsteen suffered from contractual problems that kept him from recording for 3 years in the mid-1970s. Black musicians, who historically were less savvy about contracts than their white counterparts, suffered even more. Little Richard was recently infuriated by the Disney studios' use of "Tutti Fruiti" in an animated cartoon, but was powerless to keep them from using and profiting from the song.

TEEN IDOL FROM TEXAS: BUDDY HOLLY

Born in Lubbock, Texas, in 1936, Buddy Holly led a short, 22-year life, recording a score of classic songs in a brief period from age 20 to 22. Yet few artists have had such a lasting impact on rock and roll. Holly was the first teen idol, the performer who made the rock sound acceptable to the masses.

Holly came out of a country background and grew up with the music of western swing and honky tonk (see Chapter 1). He even recorded briefly with a western-style band before forming his famous backup group, the Crickets. Holly's sound was minimal; the Crickets initially consisted of Holly on guitar, supported only by Jerry Allison's drums. Often the drummer did not even use a full kit, focusing simply on tom-toms or even hand claps. An upright bass was added, and occasionally on Crickets recordings, a second guitar. But the overall sound was one of uncluttered simplicity, with the clean guitar leads and driving drums providing the music with its raw energy.

Unlike Elvis's or Little Richards's, Holly's family life was fairly stable, and he was sociable in high school. Although he was not exceptionally popular, he certainly was not a loner. His songs reflect a happy upbringing, with lyrics centering on the trials and tribulations of being a teenager, particularly on relationships between boys and girls. In such classics as "Peggy Sue," "Everyday," When Will I Be Loved?," "Maybe Baby," and "Well Alright," Holly (and his cowriters) perfectly captured the white teen experience.

Again, it is not so much in the lyrics that Holly brought home his message, but in the sound. His vocal style, with his young boy's range, hiccups, stutters, and other childlike mannerisms, matched perfectly the youthful lyrics. Holly used repetition in his lyrics ("pretty, pretty, pretty, little Peggy Sue") and rhyme ("maybe baby, I'll be true/maybe, baby, you'll be blue") to capture the sound and feeling of young love. Although his lyrics may not have been profound, they reflected profoundly how every young teenager feels when going through first love, dating, and rejection.

Where Elvis Presley was sinister, and Little Richard manic, Buddy Holly was sweet and sincere. This image, carefully crafted on records, may not have reflected his actual performances, which were not filmed. The few TV appearances that have survived probably don't

Buddy Holly and the Crickets.
Courtesy Frank Driggs Collection

reflect what the performing band was like either. By all accounts, Holly was an energetic performer, who enjoyed ripping up the hall. By combining high energy with sweet sincerity in his music, Holly made rock more acceptable in white, middle-class homes. Many imitators who followed in the wake of Holly's tragic death in a plane accident cashed in on this new white teen audience.

Holly is probably the most often-covered performer of the 50s. Artists like Linda Ronstadt, James Taylor, and other "soft-rock" performers are constantly drawing on his repertoire. But Holly's impact was more profound than that. In the Beatles's music you can hear direct reflections of Holly in early songs like "I'll Follow the Sun" and "One After 909" (not recorded until the end of the Beatles's career). Their use of hand-clapped rhythms and simple backups is an obvious nod to Holly. American groups like Creedence Clearwater Revival drew on Holly's basic rock and roll sound to create a purely American form of Holly-influenced music. Late in his career, Holly experimented with using strings on rock records, a concept later imitated by many groups, from the Beatles ("Yesterday") on.

*   *   *   *

Elvis's, Little Richards's, and Buddy Holly's represent three different approaches to the rock medium. Each was innovative in its day, and each was highly imitated by performers who followed. These three facets of rock music—the raw sexuality of Elvis, the high energy performances of Little Richard, and the mellow sweetness of Holly—appear in the music of the next three decades. Although threre were other innovators, none could have existed without the contribution of these pioneering performers.

READ

Bleasdale, Alan, *Are You Lonesome Tonight?* London: Faber and Faber, 1985.
Goldman, Albert, *Elvis*, NY: Avon, 1982.
Tobler, John, *The Buddy Holly Story*. NY: Beaufort Books, 1983.
White, Charles, *The Life and Times of Little Richard*. NY: Pocket Books, 1985.

LISTEN

Holly, Buddy and the Crickets, *Greatest Hits*. Coral 747492.
Little Richard, *Greatest Hits*. United 7775.
———, *Well Alright*. Specialty 2136.
Presley, Elvis, *Elvis*. RCA 1254.
———, *NBC Special*. RCA 4088.
———, *The Sun Sessions*. RCA 11675.
———, *Elvis Aaron Presley*. RCA 3699.

4

Teen Idols

At a meeting in the late 1950s, the head of classical music at RCA records, addressing his peers, said: "I'm sick of Elvis Presley. RCA is a great label. We don't have to sell this so-called music to America's teens. Let's get back to producing real music." The president of RCA looked him in the eye and said, "Not a single one of your classical music records has made money for this company in years. Every one of Elvis Presley's hit records supports your music. Without Elvis, there would be no RCA today."

RCA had made an important discovery: The teen market was the most important one for records in the United States. A star like Elvis could generate enormous profits, enough to pay for groups like the Philadelphia Symphony Orchestra that cost more to record and didn't sell as many records. It wasn't long before other record companies and music publishers realized that if they wanted to stay in the music business, they would also have to exploit the teen market. This meant discovering and nurturing new recording artists, and carefully creating songs for them to perform. In the period from 1957 through 1964, an entire industry grew to profit from rock and roll.

THE BRILL BUILDING: NEW YORK'S ROCK FACTORY

By the late 1950s, there were hundreds of groups recording rock-and-roll records. Unlike later rock groups that produced their own material, members of these groups were primarily performers, not songwriters. They needed good songs that would appeal to their audience. In 1958, a guitarist named Al Nevins joined forces with a

37

promoter named Don Kirshner (1934-   ) to form Aldon Music to meet this need for new songs. Their New York City home was at 1619 Broadway in the Brill Building. They assembled a group of young, talented musicians who created some of the most memorable hits of the early 60s.

What made the "Brill Building Sound" special was the care with which the songs were crafted. Other producers tried to find good-looking performers who would appeal to teens, reasoning that if the singer was appealing to teen record buyers, the teens would purchase lots of records, regardless of the quality of the songs. For Kirshner and Nevins, the song was of primary importance. They figured that if a song was good, it would be a hit no matter who performed it. This new emphasis on songwriting laid the basis for the memorable songs written by the Beatles, Bob Dylan, and other mid-60s performers.

Several young composer/performers worked for Aldon. The first and most successful were two high school classmates from Brooklyn: Neil Sedaka (1939-   ) and Howie Greenfield. Sedaka, a high-voiced singer with well-scrubbed good looks, performed the material and wrote the music. Greenfield wrote the lyrics, focusing on topics that teens could relate to. They wrote many hits, including "Breaking Up is Hard to Do," expressing many teens' trauma over a failed relationship, through "Calendar Girl," taking the young girl through a romantic calendar of meeting, dating, and loving.

Sedaka/Greenfield were unusual members of the Aldon stable in that Sedaka actually performed their material. More typical was the then husband/wife team of Gerry Goffin (1939-   [lyrics]) and Carole King (1942-   [music]).* In about five years time, this prolific team produced about 100 hits (and 100 lesser known songs), including such classics as "Will You Love Me Tomorrow?," "Up on the Roof," and "Chains." "Will You Love Me Tomorrow?" has to be the classic expression of every teen's fear that their loved one will abandon them.

The other important composing duo in the Aldon group was Barry Mann (1939-   ) and Cynthia Weil. They wrote the most sophisticated lyrics of the group, dealing with social issues such as street-level politics ("Uptown") and drug abuse ("Kicks"). Of course,

---

*King later achieved success as a performer after she divorced Goffin. Her 1971 record, *Tapestry*, is one of the best-selling pop records of all time, and includes her hit songs "You've Got a Friend" and "I Feel the Earth Move."

the message was still presented in a marketable, highly melodic and upbeat package.

The success of Aldon was based on a simple premise: Good music will sell well. All of the Aldon composing duos wrote fine melodies. The emphasis was on upbeat tunes that anyone could sing. However, Aldon did more than just produce songs; it made demonstration records for the producers to use in making the finished recordings. In this way, it forged a sound as well as presented finished lyrics and music. And, as we have seen, the *sound* of rock music is as important as its musical content.

LIEBER, STOLLER, AND SPECTOR: THE WALL OF SOUND

The Brill Building had other tenants besides Kirshner and Nevins. Two other influential songwriters were Jerry Lieber (1933-) and Mike Stoller (1933-). They produced more soul-like material than the upbeat Aldon teams because their major client was Atlantic records, which specialized in recording black acts. Lieber and Stoller composed for most of the black vocal groups of the late 50s and early 60s, writing such classics as "Charlie Brown" (see Chapter 2) and "There Goes My Baby." They were versatile enough to work for Elvis Presley, completing the scoring of his films *Jailhouse Rock* and *King Creole*.

Lieber and Stoller are significant for having brought to New York a young composer and producer named Phil Spector. Spector was to develop into rock's most influential creative force in the early 60s. He was responsible for the famous "wall of sound," created by a new style of recording that was to be endlessly imitated.

There were certainly other important producers before Spector came on the scene. Sam Phillips (see Chapter 3) did much to create Elvis Presley's sound by choosing the backup musicians who accompanied him, selecting the songs, and even selecting the proper "take" (or performance of the song, from the many different versions that the artist recorded). But Spector was the first producer to be more important than the artists whom he produced. One hears on all of his records the stamp of his unique genius.

Spector was born in 1941 in the Bronx, New York. His family relocated to the West Coast after the death of his father, just as

Spector was entering his adolescent years. He was withdrawn as a teenager, an outcast among the blond and blue-eyed Californians. In his late-teen years, he worked his way up through the music business, performing a number of menial jobs for different record labels and producers until, in 1960, he got his chance to produce his first record. Over the next three years, he produced more hits than nearly anyone else, including 20 chart busters, among them "Then He Kissed Me," "Be My Baby," "Walking in the Rain," "You've Lost That Lovin' Feeling," and the classic "Da Doo Ron Ron."

All of these records are marked by the famous "wall of sound." Spector was able to create more densely-packed music by putting several layers of sound onto each tape. New recording equipment allowed the producer to use *multi-tracking*. In other words, he could record one musician playing one part, and then *overtrack*—or add to the basic recording—another musician playing the same part (or a slightly different part). In this way, he could create twice as much sound as could be had by just recording live. He also exercised better control over the recording, because he could *mix* the various parts, making one drummer louder or softer. If he had recorded the two musicians live, he couldn't change how the parts sounded in the finished product as easily.

Spector used multi-tracking extensively in his recordings. He added entire choirs of voices, string sections, exotic percussion instruments, and wailing horns to the basic rock combo of guitar-bass-drums. He also used echo to make the instruments sound fuller. The result was a pulsing, vibrant sound that gained the name "wall of sound" because it hit the listener with exceptional force.

Spector worked with almost all of the top vocalists of his day, but is particularly famous for his work with the so-called "girl groups." These groups of young girls, mostly teenagers themselves, perfectly expressed in their high adolescent harmonies and good-natured singing the frustration and fun of being a young girl in the early 60s. Spector is most famous for the group that he created around his wife, Ronnie, called the Ronettes. Perhaps the greatest vocalist of these groups was Darlene Love, who, as lead singer of the Crystals, recorded with Spector "Da Doo Ron Ron," and has lately made a comeback off Broadway performing songs of this era.

After the British invasion in 1964 (see Chapter 6), Spector worked sporadically, never again exhibiting the same genius as he once had. Ending a period of semireclusion, he came out of retirement to work

The Ronettes. Courtesy Frank
Driggs Collection

with such artists as John Lennon, George Harrison, and Leonard Cohen. His impact is felt on all of the pop records of the 60s, most notably in the work of Brian Wilson, who led and produced the Beach Boys (see below), and in all of the recordings made at Motown.

MANUFACTURED STARS
OF THE EARLY 60s

Once record companies discovered the teen market, it wasn't long before they began grooming talent for it. Many of these artists are truly forgettable, both as performers and as shapers of rock history. But it is important to mention a few that did have a lasting impact, if only indirectly, on rock and roll.

"Cover" Artists

In the late 1950s and early 60s, radio stations in many parts of the country that catered to white audiences were unwilling to feature black acts. Many white youths could not relate to the raw energy of a Chuck Berry, Bo Diddley, or Little Richard—or even, for that matter, to that of an Elvis, Jerry Lee Lewis, or Carl Perkins. The stations needed more conventional artists to perform the new music.

The "cover" artists were a group of white performers who adopted black rock and roll for the white audience. Often, they would not give credit to the original black artists, changing the lyrics of songs so that they would be less "offensive" to their listeners, and changing entirely the sound of the songs so that they were effectively drained of their power.

Most famous of this group was Pat Boone (1934-   ), a clean-cut singer who currently enjoys a career as an evangelist. Boone's appearances on late 50s TV variety shows, with his tie slightly askew and his hair slightly mussed, are a sad testament to an era when rock and roll was still a forbidden music in many households. Boone sang "Tutti Fruiti," but changed Little Richard's song from a celebration of teenage fun and sexuality into a dirge. Where Little Richard shouted ecstatically the nonsense chorus, Boone labored to pronounce each word, clearly singing "Tutti Fruiti, Oh Rudi" as if he were reciting a prayer.

Ironically, cover artists often scored bigger hits with the same songs than did their black counterparts. Blacks simply did not have access to the major markets where records were sold. It was easier to market a white artist. Although the cover artists did help to spread the message of rock and roll, they ultimately did more harm than good by robbing rock of its power, stealing performance opportunities from the true artists, and profiting from record sales that truly did not belong to them.

Teen Idols

Two centers of recording became important during the early 60s: New York and Los Angeles. In New York, the concept seemed to be to try recording just about anyone who might have potential. There were many small labels and many talented teens, so it was natural for many records—good, bad, and forgettable—to be cut. In Los Angeles, the record producers made more of an effort to "groom" talent, by selecting performers who they thought would appeal to a mass teen audience. Many of these performers were not great rock singers, but merely handsome young girls and boys.

Because they were the driving force behind the performers who recorded in the early 60s, we have been focusing on the songwriters and producers. In this section, we'll look at a cross-section of popular performers of the day, especially those who made the greatest contributions to the growth of rock music.

In order for stars to be made, they needed to be heard and seen. The AM radio stations (see Chapter 2) played a crucial role in bringing the rock sound to teenagers. Television and movies would play an even more important role in bringing the good-looking performers to the attention of teenagers.

The most important rock show in the 50s and 60s was Dick Clark's (1929-) *American Bandstand*, originally broadcast from Philadelphia. This show, still going strong after more than 35 years on the air, features good-looking, well-scrubbed teenagers dancing to the music of popular teen acts.

The movies brought a new type of teen film to the market. These were the so-called "beach-blanket" films, featuring the teen stars Frankie Avalon (1939-) and Annette Funicello, both of whom scored hits as pop singers. The beach-blanket films featured the slimmest of plots, centering on the exploits of a supposedly typical group of California teens as they frolicked in the sun. Avalon's endless pining for Funicello provided some love interest, and, of course, interspersed with the "action" were countless rock songs performed by the two.

Dick Clark, on the set of
"American Bandstand," c. 1956.
Courtesy Dick Clark Productions

Most of the music produced by these teen idols—Funicello, Avalon—and others—Bobby Rydell, Fabian, Bobby Vee, and Paul Anka—is forgettable. The songs were contrived to address the typical teen's fantasies and problems, but unlike the Brill Building compositions, they were mostly disposable and were performed in a style closer to that of such pop crooners as Frank Sinatra than to that of true rockers like Elvis or Buddy Holly. Funicello could barely sing, but her good looks, recognizability (she was a Mouseketeer on the famous TV show, *The Mickey Mouse Club*), and general wholesome image made her a hit.

One idol who had a similar background did have a lasting impact on rock music, however. He was Ricky Nelson (1940-1986), the son of Ozzie and Harriet Nelson. The Nelsons starred on a TV series in the 50s and 60s based on the trials and tribulations of their family life. Ozzie had been a bandleader in the 30s and 40s and was a talented musician. Ricky also was talented, and soon appeared as the somewhat rebellious teenager on the TV show, moodily strumming on his guitar. Nelson's music was inspired by rockabilly (see Chapter 1), and he scored a number of rock hits in the 50s. He made a brief comeback in the 60s, and then became a fairly successful country star. He died in a plane crash in 1986 en route to a performance.

THE PICK OF THE CROP: TRUE ARTISTS OF THE EARLY 60s

Perhaps the most original and talented of all the late 50s and early 60s stars were Don (1937-   ) and Phil (1939-   ) Everly. The Everlys are best known for their sweet, harmonic singing, which was influenced by their country upbringing. Singing in church and performing in their parents' country-and-western band, the Everlys developed a unique vocal sound that combined the smoothness of pop with the punch of rock and roll.

Their greatest hits came during a three-year period beginning in 1957 when they recorded for Cadence Records, a small independent label operating out of Nashville, Tennessee, the home of country music. Their first hit is probably their most famous song, "Bye Bye Love." The instrumental backup was minimal, emphasizing the strumming of the Everlys' two acoustic guitars, with a light accompaniment on piano, bass, and drums. This was the opposite of the "rip them up" style of a Jerry Lee Lewis or Carl Perkins. What really made this record stand out was the clarity and beauty of the vocal harmonies that seemed to float effortlessly above the accompaniment. This, along with the syncopated rhythm of the chorus, made it an immediate favorite both among country and pop audiences. It was the first true "crossover"* record.

More hits followed "Bye Bye Love," including "Wake Up, Little Susie," "[Til] I Kissed You," and "Cathy's Clown." By mid-1962, the Everlys' luck had changed, and their string of Top-10 hits ended. They struggled through the 60s, trying a variety of sounds, including pure country, country/rock, and even R&B. The brothers performed together sporadically through the 70s and early 80s, and have recently reunited for a pair of albums produced by British new-wave performer, Nick Lowe.

Instrumental Groups

A unique development of late 50s and early 60s rock music was the rise of instrumental rock groups. This is primarily due to electric guitar being used as a solo instrument in rock. Earlier in the 50s, there were R&B bands that produced instrumental records, but they featured the saxophone and the piano. Young rockers of the late 50s discovered that the guitar could be a leader too.

One contributing factor to the popularity of instrumental groups were the dance crazes that swept the country in the early 60s. The most popular of these dances was the twist, championed by singer Chubby Checker. Several variants of the twist soon developed, and other dances, with equally descriptive names, came along in rapid succession. Dancers did not require thoughtful lyrics; they simply wanted music with a good beat. This led local bands to emphasize the instrumental side of their performances.

Duane Eddy (1938-   ) is generally credited with creating the lead guitar sound that acquired the name "twangy guitar." As implied, the sound of the guitar itself—the nasal, twanging of the strings, emphasized by the distortion added by the amplifier—was behind the phrase and was the key to Eddy's success. Eddy enjoyed his

---

*"Crossover" is a term used to describe country music that incorporates elements of rock and popular music to appeal to a larger audience. It is commonly used to describe the music of Dolly Parton in the late 70s, Alabama, and Charlie Daniels.

greatest popularity in England, influencing English players such as Hank Marvin, who performed with the group the Shadows.

The most popular instrumental group of the day hailed from Seattle, Washington. They were the Ventures, and they produced many smoothly performed hits, including their big 1960 single, "Walk—Don't Run." Although disappearing quickly from the Top-40 charts, the group continued to perform well into the 70s.

Instrumentalists played a key role in a new fad that came on the scene in 1962: surf music. The "surf sound," popularized by vocalists Jan and Dean and the Beach Boys, was one of carefree fun and good times in the California sun. Hits like "Pipeline" by the Chantays and the ever-popular "Wipe Out" by the Surfaris were soon taking the national charts by storm. Although few teenagers actually got near a surfboard, they could all enjoy the vicarious thrill of surfing thanks to this new sound.

The Beach Boys

The Beach Boys began their careers as purveyors of the California good-time sound, and most of their songs centered on the life and loves of teenage surfers; however, the group matured into one of the most important in the history of American rock music.

The Beach Boys with Annette Funicello. Courtesy Frank Driggs Collection

Brian Wilson (1942-   ) was the genius behind the group's sound. He formed the band using relatives and friends to flesh out the lineup: Brian played bass; his brother Dennis (1944-1983) played drums and brother Carl (1946-   ) played lead guitar; their cousin, Mike Love, sang lead; and neighbor Al Jardine played rhythm guitar. Their first record, "Surfin'," released in 1961, sounded much like other good-time groups from the area. It featured a raunchy beat, simple instrumental accompaniment, and childlike, high vocal harmonies. This was followed by national hits "Surfin' Safari" and "Surfin' USA." With these songs, the group was already moving to the head of the surfin' sound pack.

The reason is simple. Brian, who cowrote most of the songs and arranged all of the music, was a genius for turning what could have been trite material into tight, cohesive arrangements and powerful statements. The Beach Boys sounded like they believed in what they sang, and their singing was full of such youthful energy that it doubtlessly led thousands of teens to purchase surfboards.

In the period from 1964 to 1966, Wilson reached his greatest heights of writing and arranging. The string of hits that the band produced with him—"Fun, Fun, Fun," "I Get Around," "California Girls," and "Wouldn't It Be Nice?"—have become American rock and roll classics. The vocal arrangements reached new heights of sophistication: The swirling backups on "I Get Around" transform the barbershop quartet origins of the group's style into something sophisticated and orchestral. True, the instrumental part and the lyrics of this song aren't very sophisticated, but the melding of each simple part into a cohesive whole is truly impressive. It is no wonder that these songs have survived more than 20 years.

Brian Wilson continued to work feverishly at creating increasingly complex sounds for the group. The album *Pet Sounds* from 1966 is his masterpiece; the layered instrumental sounds, unusual percussion instruments, including bicycle horns, strings, and even dogs barking, showed him to be a masterful arranger. He had withdrawn from performing, due to hearing loss, and his studio work became an obsession. From this period comes the band's last great hit, "Good Vibrations," with its swirling use of synthesizer and most complex vocal arrangement yet. The song is actually a number of short melodies put together, including the uptempo rock chorus ("Good—good—good—good vibrations") and a mellow interlude ("Goota keep those vibrations a' happening baby").

After 1968, Wilson's role in the band steadily declined as his involvement with drugs increased. In 1983, Dennis Wilson died in a swimming accident. Recently, Brian has returned to performing, along with the rest of the band. The band continues to perform; their concerts emphasize the hits of the 60s, which remain their most important contribution.

READ

Gaines, Steven, *Heroes and Villains: The True Story of the Beach Boys*. NY: New American Library, 1986.

Milward, John, *The Beach Boys Silver Anniversary*. NY: Doubleday, 1986.

Sauers, Joan, *The Everly Brothers Rock 'n' Roll*. NY: Putnam, 1986.

Williams, Richard, *Out of His Head: The Sound of Phil Spector*. NY: Outerbridge & Lazard, 1972.

LISTEN

Beach Boys, *Surfin Safari*. Capitol T 1808.

———, *Pet Sounds*. Capitol ST 2458.

———, *Greatest Hits*. Capitol ST 21628.

Eddy, Duane, *Pure Gold*. RCA ANL 2671.

Everly Brothers, *Hits*. Cadence CLP 3062.

———, *Songs Our Daddy Taught Us*. Cadence CLP 3016.

King, Carole, *Tapestry*. Ode 77009.

———, *Pearls*. Capitol 12073.

Nelson, Rick, *Story*. Ari SUS 5205.

Ronettes, *Today's Hits*. Philles 4004.

Ventures, *Walk Don't Run*. Dolton 8003.

5

Motown and Soul

Berry Gordy's Motown Records elevated black popular music to a central place in American rock history, and ended forever the segregation of black artists from the white mainstream. It is not an exaggeration to say that without Motown's contribution, it's hard to imagine the success of such artists as Michael Jackson, Prince, and Anita Baker, to name just three. This chapter will focus on the growth of the Motown sound, while taking a brief look at some of the forebears of Motown and related developments in black music.

THE FOREBEARS

Many of the black artists who influenced the growth of Motown have already been discussed in previous chapters, including Chuck Berry, Fats Domino, Little Richard, the doo wop groups, and Muddy Waters. In the mid- to late 50s, two other artists emerged who had a large impact on black music: Ray Charles and Sam Cooke.

Ray Charles

Ray Charles (born Ray Charles Robinson; 1938-   ) is one of America's greatest musical artists. Born in Albany, Georgia, Charles began to lose his eyesight early in life, and by age 7 was enrolled in a school for the blind. It is not unusual for blind children to be encouraged to be musical; at school, Charles was exposed to classical composers, while he secretly listened to jazz pianists like Art Tatum. When he was 15, he left school, and two years later traveled to Seattle, hoping to escape the racial prejudice of the South. There, he sang and played the piano in a smooth style, imitating the popular black singer, Nat "King" Cole.

It wasn't until the mid-50s that Charles discovered his natural style. At a recording session, Ray was given full artistic control to choose his accompanists, make the arrangements, and craft his own piano and vocal parts. The result was 1954's "I've Got a Woman." In it, Ray combined the exuberant, shouting style of black gospel singers with a swinging, jazzy backup, including a gospel-tinged piano part played by Charles himself. The result outraged traditionalists; bluesman Big Bill Broonzy complained: "He's mixing the blues with the spirituals. He should be singing in church."

"Mixing the blues with the spirituals" is a good, short definition of *soul*. Soul music takes the gospel sound, the deep conviction of the vocalists expressed through a shouting, raspy voice that flies from high falsetto to low bass, and weds it with secular topics: sex, intoxication, and poverty. Charles was the first great artist of soul.

Ray Charles. Courtesy Atlantic Records

But, Charles was more than that. Through the 1950s, he expanded the range of his music. Charles recorded country standards such as "I'm Movin' On," performed jazz standards at the prestigious Newport Jazz Festival, and even tackled old standards that previously no black artist would touch. Charles's liberal approach to his repertoire—and his success on the white charts—paved the way for Motown.

Sam Cooke

Sam Cooke (1931-1964) began his recording career as a gospel singer with the group the Soul Stirrers in 1951. Unlike Charles, who brought the raspy, intense gospel style to pop music, Cooke took the opposite tack: He brought the smooth, urbane style of a pop singer to gospel. Yet, even in his most polished efforts, there was an element of deep religious conviction that set his work apart.

It was only natural that a pop-based singer would reach beyond the limits of gospel. In 1957, Cooke recorded "You Send Me," his first secular release. It was an immediate sensation, and two years later Cooke signed a recording deal with RCA, the label that was so effectively promoting Elvis to white teenagers.

Although his career at RCA was spotty, Cooke achieved a remarkable string of records, particularly 1962's "Bring It On Home to Me," a duet with singer Lou Rawls. As in most of his recordings, this record featured Cooke's world-weary, sensitive, and sensuous singing. The idea that a black artist could sing in the smooth style of a white pop star was a relatively new one, and Cooke helped establish its legitimacy.

Cooke was also important because he was one of the first pop artists—black or white—who had artistic control over his records, owned his own publishing company, and operated a record label, Sar/Derby records. Bobby Womack, Billy Preston, and Lou Rawls were among the vocalists who began their careers on Sar/Derby records. This was among the first black-owned-and-operated record companies, and it laid the seeds for Motown.

MOTOWN

Motown is the capital of two of America's greatest mass-produced items: the automobile and Motown Records, the label that created popular black music for the 1960s. Like Henry Ford, Motown's founder and president, Berry Gordy (1929-   ), saw himself as providing a basic service—entertainment—to the masses. Gordy said that he was producing music for "Young America." He hoped that this youthful army of record buyers would transcend racial barriers. Armed with an excellent ear for what would be a hit, and an eye for grooming acts for the mainstream white audience, Gordy singlehandedly created a new genre that would forever carry the name of his company.

Humble Beginnings

In the mid-50s, Gordy recognized that R&B music was the wave of the future. He also realized that it was as popular among white teens as black. He began writing R&B songs as a way to break into the business. In 1957, Gordy scored his first big success with singer Jackie Wilson (1934-1984). The song, a good-natured novelty item that parodied the style of Elvis Presley, was "Reet Petite." Gordy's share in the profits was $1,000. Soon, Gordy was composing followup songs for Wilson, and as the singer's career prospered, so did Gordy's.

The seeds of the Motown sound were laid in 1959 when Gordy struck out on his own. He chose a local singer, Marv Johnson (1938-   ), for his first productions. The recordings that he made with Johnson were well arranged, simple R&B tunes. The rough edges of R&B were considerably smoothed out, however, in an attempt to appeal to both black and white audiences. The use of backup singers, including a bevy of high-voiced females and an energetic male bass, is a typical Gordy touch.

In 1959, Gordy formed his first label, Tammie Records (he soon changed the name to Tamla). He was fortunate in his first major discovery, a local vocal group called the Miracles, featuring four men and a woman. The lead singer for the Miracles was a sweet-voiced young black man who was also a talented songwriter. His name was Smokey Robinson (1940-   ). The Miracles's second single was a song written by Robinson called "Shop Around," which reached Number 2 on the pop charts. Motown was on the road to success.

Motown Records made its home in a tiny bungalow in Detroit, with the words "HITSVILLE U.S.A." emblazoned on a large sign. Gordy hired Robinson as his first house songwriter, and soon added to the stable a talented house band, and a number of successful songwriters and producers. Motown became a factory into which

Gordy fed the raw talent of Detroit's streets and out of which came stars who could perform on any stage, from Harlem's Apollo Theatre to the palaces of Las Vegas.

The Golden Years

The key to Gordy's success was in his total control of the music that Motown produced. Certainly, he was lucky in discovering some of the greatest black performers of our time, performers like Robinson, Diana Ross and the Supremes, Stevie Wonder, Marvin Gaye, the Four Tops, the Temptations, Gladys Knight, and Michael Jackson and the Jackson Five. But talent alone was not what put Motown over the top.

The first important ingredient was the songs themselves. Like Chuck Berry, Gordy produced songs that would appeal to all teenagers, black and white. Although some songs reflected black concerns, such as poverty and race relations, most expressed more general concerns, and could apply to any teen. The spurned lover, the lonely teen, jealousy, and difficulties catching boys or winning girls were typical Motown subjects.

Beyond the subjects, the songs were carefully crafted. The most famous Motown songsmiths were Brian Holland (1941-), Lamont Dozier (1941-), and Eddie Holland (1939-). This team's first hit was "Heat Wave," recorded in 1963 by Martha and the Vandellas. The song is typical Motown. Unlike earlier pop songs that feature verse-chorus-verse-chorus and so on, or even verse-chorus-bridge, "Heat Wave" is based on short phrases that are repeated throughout the song. The result is a more tightly structured song having greater impact on the listener.

The Motown band was another important ingredient in the overall sound. Although occasionally producers added interesting touches, such as unusual percussion instruments, strings, or brass, the key to the success of the Motown sound can be expressed in one word: simplicity. Unlike bands from other studios, the Motown band strove for and achieved anonymity. A simple drums-bass-guitar backup was all that was needed.

Finally, Motown was able to offer listeners a seemingly endless variety of moods from the vast stable of acts under contract to the label. Each group was carefully groomed to have its own identity. The Four Tops were structured around the magnificent vocals of group leader Levi Stubbs, who sounds like a cross between a preacher and a blues growler. Stubbs tirelessly screamed, begged, howled, and growled. With songs like "Baby I Need Your Loving," "I Can't Help Myself," and "I'll Be There," the Tops achieved lasting fame in the years 1964-66.

The lushly romantic Miracles, led by silky voiced Smokey Robinson, represented the other end of the spectrum from the Tops. Although Smokey could write upbeat numbers like "Shop Around," he was most comfortable composing and singing ballads. The Miracles's greatest hit of this genre was 1965's "The Tracks of My Tears." In this classic song, Smokey used his voice to express the pathos of every teenager's feelings of rejection by a loved one.

Motown's other great male vocal group was the Temptations. Unlike the Miracles and the Four Tops, the Temptations did not have a single vocalist who stood out from the rest. Rather, they excelled at ensemble work. The quality of vocalists, from shimmering tenor to booming bass, sets their work apart. They were also talented dancers; every move of the ensemble was carefully choreographed. They are most famous for "My Girl," written for them by Smokey Robinson and recorded in 1965.

The Temptations. Courtesy Frank Driggs Collection

Motown also nurtured several great female vocalists. Martha Reeves (1941-), of Martha and the Vandellas, was dicovered by Gordy in the Motown office working as a secretary. She was a live wire, and the songs written for her reflected her unbridled energy. Her greatest hit was "Heat Wave," followed by the 1960s anthem, "Dancin' in the Streets."

Perhaps the greatest Motown group was the Supremes, three Detroit teenagers who were molded into superstars by Gordy. The girls were sent to the Motown finishing school, where they learned to dance, dress, speak and move like young ladies. Gordy quickly chose Diana Ross (1944-) to lead the group, primarily because of her looks and general demeanor.*

The Supremes. Courtesy Frank Driggs Collection

The Supremes's first big hit was 1964's "Where Did Our Love Go?" For the next five years, they were the most successful female group in the history of rock and roll. Their next five singles were all Number-1 hits, and they were to record seven more Number-1 songs before disbanding in 1969.

---

*The other two original Supremes were Mary Wilson (1944-) and Florence Ballard (1943-1976). Cindy Birdsong replaced Ballard in 1967.

The key to the group's success was the excellence of their songs, many of which were written by Holland-Dozier-Holland (including classics like "You Keep Me Hanging On," "Stop in the Name of Love," "Baby Love," and "Love Child"), and Ross's lead vocals. Ross's girlish vocals and coy good looks made her instantly popular on television and in fancy clubs. The Supremes were notable not only for their singing but also their fashions; they wore a variety of wigs, while they toted an entire wardrobe drawn from the latest styles.

Later in the 60s, another important female singer came to the fore: Gladys Knight (1944-   ), backed by a family group called the Pips. Knight's background was in gospel, having recorded with two religious groups before switching to secular material. Motown capitalized on her gritty vocals in the original version of "I Heard It Through the Grapevine" (1967; further popularized by Marvin Gaye, see below) and "If I Were Your Woman" (1970).

As the 60s came to a close, Motown began to lose its iron grip on the pop charts. Some artists on the label gained more freedom. Marvin Gaye (1939-1984) broke the Motown mold. He began his career as a drummer, but soon established himself as a sexy, powerful singer. He scored several hits singing duets with Tammie Terrell, including love songs by songwriters Ashford and Simpson. His greatest hit of the 60s was 1968's "I Heard It Through the Grapevine," a song of great power that expresses more than its lyrics suggest. Gaye's brilliant vocal, moving effortlessly from soft brooding to shouting intensity, paired with a repeated chorus sung by background singers and a spooky electric piano part, makes it one of the most interesting of all of Motown's pop classics.

In 1971, Gaye produced and composed an entire album, shunning the house composers and typical Motown backup band. The songs commented on contemporary issues, including black activism, the Vietnam war, and air and water pollution. This landmark collection—appropriately called *What's Going On?*—broadened the range of topics that a popular black singer could address. Later in the 70s, Gaye again surprised his fans by championing sexual freedom as a means of achieving personal growth, recording "Let's Get it On" (1973) and the erotic "Sexual Healing" (1982). Tragically, Gaye was shot by his father just as he was making a comeback in the early 1980s.

The second renegade Motown artist began his career as a young boy. Born in 1950, Steveland Morris was discovered by one of the singers in the Miracles when he was 10 years old. The child sang, played the harmonica, and danced up a storm. Renamed Little Stevie Wonder, his first hit was 1963's "Fingertips Part 2." Soon, Stevie was in demand on network TV and in concert as the boy wonder of the harmonica.

Not content with remaining a novelty artist, Wonder learned other instruments, including synthesizers, and studied recording technology. By the early 1970s, Stevie was ready to assert his independence. He was the first Motown artist to sign a contract giving him complete control over his records. The albums that he produced—*Music of My Mind*, *Talking Book* (in 1972), *Innervisions* (1973) and *Songs in the Key of Life* (1976)—showed his true genius. Wonder composed, arranged, and performed all of his music by overtracking a variety of keyboards, including organ, clavinet, piano, and synthesizers. The result was a unique sound that was also commercial.

Wonder continues to evolve as an artist, composing film scores and theme albums, such as the recently released album *Characters*, commenting on contemporary political figures.

One of the last great acts signed by Motown in the 60s was the Jackson Five, a family group discovered by Diana Ross while performing in their hometown of Gary, Indiana. Michael Jackson (1959-   ) was 10 years old when he sang lead on the group's first single, the upbeat funk number "I Want You Back." His acrobatic dancing, derived from performers like James Brown (see below), and energetic singing set the song apart. Gordy dressed the group in wildly colored clothes and exaggerated hats. Songs were chosen to appeal to preteens, like "ABC," and a cartoon show was developed to exploit their popularity with young audiences. A decade later, Michael Jackson emerged as one of rock's great performers, producing the landmark *Thriller* and *Bad* albums, with a series of videos that elevated rock dancing to new heights.

SOUL

Soul singers took the enthusiasm and deep feeling of gospel music and brought it to pop songs. While Motown Records was the label that attempted to introduce black artists to a white audience, the soul singers primarily performed for labels geared to a black market. The most famous record label specializing in soul was Stax Records, based in Memphis, Tennessee.

The house band at Stax, Booker T. and the MGs, gained fame and fortune on their own as a powerful combo. It is also noteworthy that the band was biracial, including two black musicians, leader Booker T. Jones (1944-   ) and drummer Al Jackson, Jr. (1934-1975), and two whites, Steve Cropper (1941-   ) on guitar and Donald "Duck" Dunn (1941-   ) on bass. The MGs surpassed the venerable Tijuana Brass in instrumental hits in their greatest year, 1967. Other Stax artists included Otis Redding, Isaac Hayes, and the vocal duo Sam and Dave, whose hit "Soul Man" defined the soul sound.

The most influential soul artist was the man who gained the nickname "The Godfather of Soul," James Brown. Brown was born in 1928, and scored his first big hit in 1956 with the single "Please, Please, Please." This record set the style for all of Brown's work that followed. Brown shouted the lyrics as if he were transported by his feelings. This vocal style recalled the sound of a black Holy Roller preacher calling on his congregation to reform their wicked ways. Brown's stage show was the most flamboyant since Little Richard's or Jerry Lee Lewis's. He aimed to have the loudest band, the flashiest clothes, the most acrobatics, and the most outrageous hairstyle of any performer on the road. His sidemen would often escort the exhausted singer off stage, draped in regal purple robes.

Brown's musical accompaniment was also revolutionary. His backup band emphasized rhythm over melody or even harmony. The guitarist held his fretting hand across the strings in order to "choke" the sound of a chord. Meanwhile, he would strum energetically across the strings with his picking hand, creating a sound not unlike a quickly repeated rifle shot. At key moments in a song, a group of horns would break in to punctuate the rhythm with a shot of powerful sound. The bass player created his own rhythmic part, playing broken patterns against the incessant beat of the guitars. Brown came the closest to creating African *polyrhythms* (or more than one rhythm being performed at once) in contemporary pop music than any other performer.

Two female vocalists reigned as queens of soul in the 60s: Aretha Franklin and Tina Turner. Franklin (1942-   ) came out of a gospel tradition, and applied this to the music that made her famous in the mid-60s. Aretha took to the road at the age of 14 with her father, the Reverend C. L. Franklin, who led a number of evangelical crusades.

Aretha Franklin. Courtesy Atlantic
Records

In the early 60s, she was signed to Columbia Records, a company that did not have a good grasp on the black market. She recorded gospel, blues, and jazz numbers, but never really found her own sound. It was not until she moved to Atlantic Records, a label sympathetic to and understanding of black artists, that her career flourished.

Aretha's greatest hit was "Respect," a song originally recorded by soul singer Otis Redding (1941-1967). Other hits included "I Never Loved A Man (The Way I Love You)," which featured Aretha's own gospel-tinged piano playing, and the classic "[You Make Me Feel Like] A Natural Woman." Aretha was nicknamed "Lady Soul," and in the period of 1967 to 1974, she scored the most Top-10 hits of any black singer, with the exception of James Brown. Recently, she has had several hit singles, including "Freeway of Love."

The other great female soul singer of the 60s was Tina Turner (b. Anna Mae Bullock; 1939-   ). The daughter of a sharecropper in rural Tennessee, Tina was discovered by blues pianist/promoter Izear Luster ("Ike"; 1931-   ) Turner, a talent scout and record producer for many small labels. Ike formed the Ike and Tina Turner Review, and penned their first hit, 1960's "A Fool in Love."

The Review spotlighted Tina's outrageous performances. She wore elaborate wigs and short-short dresses, high-heel pumps and black fishnet stockings. Tina danced energetically and shouted enthusiastically as she sang. The spectacle was completed by the singing Ikettes, good-looking women who danced and sang backup vocals. The duo's greatest hits were the Phil-Spector-produced "River Deep—Mountain High" (1966) and "Proud Mary" (1969).

Tina's singing style, like Aretha's, shows intensity and passion, a raw power that far surpasses the coy girlishness of Diana Ross. Her ability to survive—Tina was controlled and mercilessly beaten by Ike during their years of marriage—has been an inspiration to women everywhere, black and white. Tina made a triumphant comeback in 1984 with her *Private Dancer* album, opening the door for renewed recognition of Aretha and other black soul singers.

READ

Benjamin, Peter, *The Story of Motown*. NY: Grove Press, 1979.

Brown, Geoffrey, *Diana Ross*. NY: St. Martins, 1981.

Charles, Ray and David Ritz, *Brother Ray*. NY: Warner Books, 1979.

Mabery, D. L., *Tina Turner*. Minneapolis, MN: Lerner Publications, 1986.

Shaw, Arnold, *Black Popular Music in America*. NY: Schirmer Books, 1986.

———, *Honkers and Shouters: The Golden Years of Rhythm and Blues*. NY: Collier Books,

Wilson, Mary, *Dreamgirl: My Life as a Supreme*. NY: St. Martins, 1986.

LISTEN

Booker T. and the MGs, *Best Of*. Stax 8202.

Brown, James, *Unbeatable Hits*. King 919.

———, *Papa's Got a Brand New Bag*. King 938.

Charles, Ray, *Ray Charles*. Atlantic 8006.

———, *Genius Of*. Atlantic 1312.

———, *Modern Sounds in C & W*. ABC 410.

Cooke, Sam, *16 Greatest Hits*. Trip 152.

Franklin, Aretha, *Lady Soul*. Atlantic 8176.

———, *Aretha Gold*. Atlantic 8227.

Gaye, Marvin, *How Sweet It Is*. Motown 258.

——— and Tammy Terrell, *United*. Motown 277.

———, *What's Going On?* Motown 310.

Jackson Five, *Greatest Hits*. Motown 741.

Jackson, Michael, *Thriller*. Epic QE 38112.

Martha and the Vandellas, *Heat Wave*. Gordy 907.

Robinson, Smokey and the Miracles, *Shop Around*. Motown 224.

———, *Greatest Hits*. Tamla 254.

Supremes, *Sing Holland-Dozier-Holland*. Motown 650.

———, *Anthology*. Motown 774.

Temptations, *Greatest Hits*. Warner Brothers 1810.

Turner, Ike and Tina, *Greatest Hits*. Warner Brothers 1810.

Turner, Tina, *Private Dancer*. Capitol 512330.

Wonder, Stevie, *Music of My Mind*. Motown 314.

———, *Talking Book*. Motown 319.

———, *Innervisions*. Motown 326

———, *Anthology*. Motown 804.

———, *Songs in the Key of Life*. Motown 340.

6

The British Invasion

In 1964, four young "lads" from Liverpool changed the direction of rock music. Their group was called the Beatles, and the songs that they wrote, the sounds that they created, even the way they wore their hair, changed the direction of American culture. In the same year, a rougher looking group of young men from London were also making inroads into America. This group, known as the Rolling Stones in honor of American bluesman Muddy Waters (see Chapter 1), were also enormously influential in shaping rock and roll.

THE BEATLES

The Beatles (John Lennon, Paul McCartney, George Harrison, and Richard Starkey [Ringo Starr]) were born in Liverpool, England, a seaport on the west coast of the country. In the years following World War II, Liverpool became an important center of trade. Sailors were constantly coming in and out of the port town, and they brought with them recordings of music that they had purchased in America. Country stars such as Hank Williams and R&B performers like Chuck Berry and Little Richard were not unknown to the Liverpool population.

In postwar England, American music was extremely popular. Jazz from the 20s, 30s, and 40s, which the English dubbed "Trad Jazz," could be heard in many clubs. American folk music was also popular, particularly the music of black guitarists. The English melded these two musical influences into a new form and called it "skiffle." Skiffle bands featured guitars, washtub bass,* tenor banjo and other rhythm instruments, and percussion.

John Lennon (1940-1980), who founded the Beatles, formed his first band while attending Quarry Bank School. He named the group the Quarrymen, after his alma mater. The group played mostly skiffle music, and performed at local functions. Lennon was influenced in his dress and performance by his idol, American rock star Elvis Presley. He wore his hair in an upturned wave, sported a leather jacket, and tried his best to sneer at the audience like Elvis.

At one local performance, Lennon was introduced to a talented left-hand guitarist. What impressed him most about James Paul McCartney (1942-) was his ability to mimic riffs from his favorite rock records. Paul could also imitate the wild, high-pitched screams of Little Richard. Soon, Paul was a member of the band.

A scruffy, acne-scarred teenager named George Harrison (1943-) befriended John and Paul. Although the two older boys found him hopelessly immature at first, they admired his guitar skills. George was a fan of guitarist Scotty Moore (who backed Elvis), and through hours of listening to Elvis's records he had perfected many of Scotty's licks. In 1958, the young guitarist was enlisted into the group, which performed under a number of names, including Johnny and the Moondogs and Long John and the Silver Beetles (the "beetles" was selected in honor of the Crickets, who backed up Buddy Holly). The idea of changing the spelling to b-e-a-t-l-e-s was John's; it was a pun, indicating the band's allegiance to music with a beat.

In 1959, long-time Lennon friend Stu Sutcliffe (1940-1962) joined the group as bass player, and in 1960, Pete Best (1941-), a good-looking young man whose mother owned a local club where the group performed, joined on drums. In the same year, the group made their first trip to Hamburg, Germany.

Hamburg was the home of a number of seedy clubs where English-speaking bands performed for audiences of sailors, whores, and students who enjoyed mixing with the local lowlifes. At the clubs, the Beatles learned how to play for hours, mastering everything from old standards like "My Bonnie Lies Over the Ocean" and "A Taste of Honey" to raucous rockers. Group members were also introduced to

---

* A homemade bass guitar, made from a piece of heavy twine, attached to a stick that is anchored to an upside-down washtub, that serves as a resonator.

"pep pills," or speed, as a means of coping with the long hours of performing.

The trips to Hamburg enhanced the group's reputation, and in 1961 they landed a recording contract as a backup band for pop singer Tony Sheridan. Sheridan was a rock crooner in the style of the American teen idols (see Chapter 4), and the recordings he made with the Beatles were not terribly exciting.

On their return to Liverpool, the Beatles continued performing in a number of local clubs. They became the favorite noon-hour band at the Cavern Club, a local hole-in-the-wall where teens flocked to hear the new rock and roll. Still, despite winning considerable local fame, the Beatles were making little progress toward their ultimate goal. Lennon dreamed of reaching "the toppermost of the poppermost," as he was fond of saying. His goal was to be more famous than Elvis. He could hardly imagine how, in a few short years, the group would achieve this goal and more.

One day in November 1961, Brian Epstein (1934-1967) came to hear the Beatles perform at the Cavern Club. He came from a well-to-do family that operated a large furniture store in Liverpool. Epstein, who headed the store's record department, had received many requests from teenagers for an obscure record that featured a local band called the Beatles. He decided to hear this band for himself, and

The Beatles. Courtesy Frank Driggs Collection

ventured into the strange world of a rock club. What he saw fascinated him. The raw energy and power of the performers, along with the sarcastic quick wit of leader Lennon, impressed him.

Epstein quickly signed on as the group's manager. After a number of failed attempts to sell his group to London's recording executives, Epstein played an audition tape for George Martin (1926-   ) at the tiny Parlophone label. Martin had previously recorded comedy records; his knowledge of rock, like Epstein's, was limited. But he decided to take a risk with the Beatles.

When the Beatles came to London to record, the band was a quartet. Stu Sutcliffe had left the band in Germany when he fell in love with a local artist; soon thereafter, he died of a brain tumor. McCartney had taken over his role as bass player. Just before their recording contract was finalized, Pete Best was replaced by Richard Starkey (1940-   ), a seasoned Liverpool drummer. His love of rings gained him the nickname Ringo Starr. The final Beatles lineup was Lennon on lead vocals and rhythm guitar, McCartney on lead vocals and bass, Harrison on harmony vocals and lead guitar, and Starr on occasional vocals and drums. Lennon also played harmonica on some early sessions, and both he and McCartney played piano.

The group was brought to Parlophone's studios in August 1962. At first, Martin was discouraged by the group's self-composed songs. He just didn't feel there was anything strong enough to record. He particularly disliked a slow country number, penned by Lennon and McCartney in 1957 and featuring Lennon's harmonica playing, called "Love Me Do." He insisted that the band record a professionally composed song for their first single, and they dutifully recorded "How Do You Do?," a trite love song. However, John and Paul worked hard at improving "Love Me Do," and finally, after speeding up its tempo and reworking the arrangement, Martin decided to release this as their first single. The song peaked at number 21 on the British charts.

The Beatles's second song fared better. A song with clever lyrics written by Lennon, "Please Please Me" had a catchy melody that was enhanced by Martin's arrangement. The driving drum beat, the insistent repetition of "C,mon, c'mon . . . c'mon, c'mon," and McCartney's falsetto, came together to make an overall sound that was bright and happy. The song reached Number 1 on the British charts. An album was quickly recorded to meet the demand for more Beatles music, and was equally successful.

1963 was the year that the Beatles took England by storm. Epstein cleverly built on the group's popularity. He dressed them in collarless suits and high-topped boots. Epstein cleaned up their stage act, creating their famous low bow, in which all four members took a distinguished formal bow at the end of each number. The famous Beatles haircut replaced the early, greasy 50s look. This style actually came about by accident. George Harrison went swimming one day and forgot to take along a comb. The result was long bangs that hung over his forehead. The rest of the group was impressed with the look, and soon everyone in England was letting their hair grow long.

Oddly enough, their success in England was not immediately repeated in the United States. Capitol, Parlophone's sister label in the United States, had turned down the chance to release their records. Epstein went to work, pestering the United States label to do something for his boys. The result was a mass-media campaign in early 1964 to introduce the Beatles's next single, "I Want to Hold Your Hand." In February of that year, the Beatles arrived in the United States and appeared on the *Ed Sullivan Show*, the most-watched variety show on television at the time. The result was an immediate outbreak of "Beatlemania." The American teen market was ecstatic over these good-looking, well-scrubbed British youths.

"I Want to Hold Your Hand" does not have profound lyrics or an elaborate melody. In later years, both Lennon and McCartney commented that they were uninterested in the small details, such as individual words or phrases. Instead, they hoped to craft a new sound, something that would be distinctly their own. Martin's genius in the studio, coupled with the infectious harmonies, lively playing, and innovative song structures that the quartet created, set the Beatles's songs apart.

The selection of songs on the group's first few albums was divided between recreations of classic rock songs and original compositions. Although they idolized Chuck Berry, Little Richard, and Elvis Presley, they did not try to imitate their sounds. Paul could certainly scream like Little Richard on "Long Tall Sally," but no one would mistake him for an American black. In fact, one of the Beatles's contributions to English music was that they were proud of being Liverpudlians. By being themselves, they showed other English performers how they could create new music while drawing on American roots.

By mid-1965, the Beatles were seasoned stars, with more Number-1 hits under their belts than groups that had been recording for decades, rather than just three years. They had appeared in two movies, *A Hard Day's Night* and *Help*, which set new standards for rock and roll films. The group was also maturing as recording artists. John Lennon had become a fan of Bob Dylan, the American singer-songwriter who introduced serious topics to popular music (see Chapter 7). Lennon began to write more serious lyrics and complex melodies. He would soon be using revolutionary studio techniques, such as adding a section of tape running backwards to the end of the song "Rain" to create an eerie coda.

McCartney, meanwhile, was blossoming into a major pop songwriter. Unlike Lennon, who was exploring more personal issues, McCartney crafted songs that ran the gamut from hard rock to romantic ballads. His greatest achievement was 1966's "Yesterday." The recording of "Yesterday" was revolutionary; instead of the full band, Martin recorded McCartney singing alone to an acoustic guitar accompaniment, and then added a tasteful string quartet. This arrangement has been copied countless times by other artists and producers.

By 1966, the Beatles were cultural heroes as well as pop artists. Their every word was analyzed. Lennon, in an interview, noted ironically that more young people were inspired by the Beatles than by God. This off-the-cuff statement, which was widely misquoted to say that Lennon thought the Beatles were *better* than God, enraged religious fundamentalists in the United States. Public burnings of Beatles records were common in the second half of 1966.

By the end of the year, the pop group made the unprecedented decision to stop touring and to focus on their studio work. Previously, rock bands lived by touring. Tours helped sell records, and brought the bands to their fans. The Beatles's tours, though, had become increasingly difficult. The fans screamed so loudly that the performers could not hear themselves playing. As the Beatles's work matured, they found it increasingly difficult to play their complicated musical arrangements in large arenas filled with screaming teenage girls.

In 1967, the band recorded their most influential single, "Strawberry Fields Forever/Penny Lane," and their greatest album, *Sergeant Pepper's Lonely Hearts Club Band*. The single recalled Lennon's and McCartney's childhood. Lennon created an aural picture of his childhood in "Strawberry Fields" by overtracking two different versions of the song. His voice took on a sleepy, unearthly quality, because the two different vocal versions that were placed on top of each other ran at slightly different speeds. The use of unusual musical instruments, backward-running tape, and a montage of sound added to a total musical experience that was unprecedented in pop music.

McCartney's contribution, "Penny Lane," was typically brighter, more solidly in the pop mold. But even so, the use of a baroque trumpet, inspired by Bach's Brandenburg concerti, is an unusual touch for a pop song. The song's story line is almost surrealistic, as characters come and go and the narrator, strangely detached and amused, recounts how their actions overlap.

Sergeant Pepper's is perhaps the most celebrated album in all pop music. Everything, from the elaborate cover art to the programming of the songs, was carefully planned. Previously, albums had merely been collections of hit singles, and so could be very uneven. Now, the Beatles approached the album format as a work of art. They recreated themselves as the mythical "Sergeant Pepper Band," introducing audience sound effects after the first song. They shortened the space between the songs so that each piece ran into the next. The arrangements were complex, calling for almost every instrument in the orchestra, and some from other cultures, such as the Indian *sitar* (lute) and *tabla* (drums).

The most celebrated song from this album was "A Day in the Life," a song that was banned in England. Composed in sections by Lennon and McCartney, the song recounts the day of an "average" citizen. Lennon's ironic detachment as he repeats horrible occurrences that he has read in the paper alternates with McCartney's cheerful recounting of a typical morning as a young businessman rushes off to work. The song incorporates the sounds of the day—an alarm clock, the huffing and puffing of the rushing worker, the babble of voices heard on the streets—as well as pure sounds. The song ends with the rushing sound of an orchestra progressing up the scale to a triumphant final chord. This is rock music at its most complex.

After this album was released, the Beatles began to grow apart. Lennon had befriended conceptual artist and musician Yoko Ono, who was to become his second wife. Harrison became a follower of the Maharishi Mahesh Yogi, an Indian mystic, and convinced other group members to follow him on a pilgrimage to India in 1968. The group experienced a devastating blow when manager Brian Epstein was found dead of an overdose of bartiturates. Although they continued to produce innovative music—including the landmark single "Hey Jude" in 1968, which ran over seven minutes—four minutes longer than the average rock song—they worked increasingly as solo artists, drawing on the others to back them up as needed, rather than as a band.

The Beatles disbanded in 1969. The greatest and most revolutionary rock band of all time, which had recorded for only seven years, was no more, but their recordings continue to influence rock music today.

THE ROLLING STONES: BAD BOYS OF ROCK AND ROLL

The Beatles took their inspiration from American pop rock, from Elvis and Chuck Berry and Buddy Holly; the Rolling Stones drew from a deeper vein of American music, from the urban blues of Muddy Waters, Howlin' Wolf, and B. B. King (see Chapter 1). While the Beatles were safe enough for American television, the Stones always projected danger and rebellion, which meant to scare Mom and Dad—while winning the hearts of America's teens.

The Stones had their roots in the British blues revival that occurred in the early 60s in London, centering on a club run by blues singer Alex Korner. Their leader was Brian Jones (1942-1969), an extraordinarily gifted musician, a golden-haired guitarist who was the best-looking of a scruffy-looking group. The second guitarist was Keith Richards (1942-   ), a fan of Chuck Berry, who played lead guitar to Jones's rhythm parts. Vocalist Mick Jagger (1943-   ) was initially a shy young man, embarrassed by his exaggerated lips and unusual looks that had made him less than a lady killer in high school. The group was rounded out by bass player Bill Wyman (1936-   ), a morose looking young man who was part of the growing blues scene, and drummer Charlie Watts (1941-   ), a seasoned professional whose first love was jazz.

Unlike the Beatles, three of the Stones's roots were in the English middle class. Jones, Jagger, and Richards—the heart of the creative end of the group—came from suburban London, a far more cosmopolitan city than Liverpool. They were well educated; Jagger studied at the London School of Economics, a prestigious business school, and did not abandon his school career until 1963. In the period 1961-63, band members undoubtedly viewed the whole venture as merely another outgrowth of the blues scene. While they were happy to play local clubs, they were not looking for careers in music.

The Stones's first big break came in 1963, when they scored a hit with—oddly enough—a leftover Lennon/McCartney composition, "I

Want to Be Your Man." Meeting the two young composers from the Beatles convinced Jagger and Richards that they too could write original songs. It also led to a continuing rivalry between the Beatles and Stones that would last throughout the 60s, as each group tried to top the others' successes.

Also in 1963, Andrew Loog Oldham, a young, hip member of London's growing class of artists, promoters, and musicians, took on the job of managing the Stones. Unlike Brian Epstein, who had little experience in the world of pop music, Oldham clearly saw how the Stones could be molded into major figures in the British pop scene. He capitalized on their reputation of being bad boys, playing on the natural tendency of teens to be rebellious. Oldham also served as the group's producer in the recording studio, giving them unusual freedom to mold their own sound.

The Stones from the start took an educated approach to their music. Jagger, Richards, and Jones were avid record collectors. They were not content to perform cover versions of well-known R&B songs; they sought out unusual songs, songs that were barely known in America, let along the United Kingdom. Although the Stones loved black American R&B, they also were aware that they were not black or American. Also, they wanted to be successful, and realized that not all teenagers were ready for purely raw blues. Jagger imitated the singing style of American blacks, slurring his words, shouting and moaning, suggesting a strong sexual energy. At the same time, to point out the fact that he wasn't the howling bluesman that he so artfully imitated, he seemed to mock himself by overdoing these mannerisms.

The Stones's first big American hit came in the summer of 1965: the Jagger/Richards song "[I Can't Get No] Satisfaction." Based on a simple guitar riff, the story line was purposely difficult to understand. While the singer complains, over and over, that "I can't get no . . . I can't get no . . . I can't get no . . . Sat-is-faction," exactly *what* he is seeking is left undefined. The music itself implies freedom, rebellion, and sex, but the words carefully avoid taking any direct stand. This is typical of the Stones; they want both to rebell and make it big on the pop charts.

"Satisfaction" was followed by a string of hits that expressed similar tension between raw power and ambiguous feeling. "Paint it Black" is, presumably, about the singer's need to remove every positive feeling from his life and to live only in the darkness. Again, though, it is the sound of the song that remains with the listener as strongly as the lyric. Jagger's suggestive moaning at the end of the song—accompanied by Jones's innovative sitar playing and the use of exotic drums—is perhaps as meaningful as the lyrics.

Other songs from this period expressed the Stones's infamous contempt for women. "Under My Thumb" is the typical fantasy of a young boy who has been dominated by a woman through his desire for her. Now, he is able to boast that he is able to control her: "Under my thumb, is a girl who once held me down . . ." Another song that expresses contempt for women is "Mother's Little Helper."

In the later 60s, the Stones's sound grew increasingly complex. Oldham ceased serving as their manager/producer in 1967; they no longer needed his help in fostering a bad boy image. Meanwhile, the Beatles's use of increasingly complex studio sounds, orchestral instruments, and deeper lyrics led the Stones themselves to dabble in what has been called "psychedelic rock." This music, influenced by drugs, "happenings" in the art and theater world of London, and Indian music and religion, shows itself in the Stones's most elaborately conceived album, *Their Satanic Majesties Request*, and the song "She's a Rainbow."

In the years 1967-69, Brian Jones retreated increasingly into his own world. He experimented with unusual musical instruments, and brought his wide knowledge of sounds and styles to the Stones's music. Meanwhile, an increasing dependency on drugs led him to be

The Rolling Stones. Courtesy Frank Driggs Collection

a less influential member in terms of the band's overall growth. Jagger and Richards were the songwriters, so their influence was becoming increasingly strong. It was clear that they did not enjoy sharing the spotlight with Jones. It is also clear that, although Jagger sympathized with the artistic innovations of the 60s, he was also interested in continuing to make hit records. As a businessman, he could see that Jones was no longer useful in the group. Just as Jones was being edged out of the group, he retreated further into drug dependency, and died in a swimming pool accident on July 3, 1969.

From the late 60s on, the Stones returned to a more simple, roots-oriented sound. They recorded several basic rock numbers that have become standards, including "Honky Tonk Woman" and "Jumpin' Jack Flash." It can be argued that these songs aren't really about anything. Jagger himself has commented that he often mumbled the lyrics because the lyrics weren't terribly important. The sound and the beat bear the message, as much as the catchphrases such as "It's a gas, gas, gas" from "Jumpin' Jack Flash."

The Stones's rebellious image fit in well with the free-living style of San Francisco, where they were idolized by both the peace-loving hippies and the Hell's Angels, a motorcycle gang. The Stones performed for a crowd of 300,000 of their devoted California fans at an automobile raceway in Altamount in the summer of 1969; the result was an infamous disaster in which the Angels murdered one crowd member, and three others were killed in the chaos that followed. Jagger, Richards, and company were brought face to face with the consequences of the deadly image that they had contrived.

Still, the Stones managed to survive this tragedy and continue to make music. In the mid-70s, the group lagged as Richards struggled with drug addiction, and Jagger entered the world of high society. A comeback began in 1978 with the album *Some Girls*, and continued unabated through this year. Large stadium tours, hit records, and the sight of 40-plus-year-old Britains still rocking and rolling helped secure their place in rock history for a new generation. Lately, Jagger has been pursuing solo projects and expressing dissatisfaction with the Stones's continued emphasis on roots rock. Meanwhile, drummer Charlie Watts has branched out to perform with a 40-piece jazz band; bassist Wyman has scored films; and new guitarist, Ron Wood, and Richards served as backup musicians for Aretha Franklin and Bob Dylan.

Although it is unclear whether the Stones still will be rolling in their 60s, 70s, and 80s, it is clear that every rock group—from heavy metalists like Van Halen to soft rockers like the Eagles—owe something to the ground that they broke.

READ

Aftel, Mandy, *Death of a Rolling Stone*. NY: Delilah Books, 1982.

Booth, Stanley, *Dance with the Devil*. NY: Random House, 1984.

Brown, Peter and Steven Gaines, *The Love You Make*. NY: New American Library, 1984.

Guillano, Geoffrey, *The Beatles: A Celebration*. NY: St. Martins, 1986.

Hampton, Wayne, *Guerilla Minstrels: John Lennon, Joe Hill, Woody Guthrie, and Bob Dylan*. Knoxville: University of Tennessee, 1986.

Hoffman, Dezo, *The Rolling Stones: The Early Years*. NY: McGraw-Hill, 1985.

Norman, Philip, *Shout!* NY: Simon and Schuster, 1981.

————, *Symphony for the Devil*. NY: Simon and Schuster, 1984.

Stokes, Geoffrey, *The Beatles*. NY: Times Books, 1980.

Wenner, Jann, *Lennon Remembers*. NY: Fawcett, 1972.

LISTEN

Beatles, *Introducing the Beatles*. Vee Jay SR 1062.

————, *Meet the Beatles*. Capitol 2047.

————, *Hard Day's Night*. United Artists 3366 64.

————, *Help*. Capitol 2386.

————, *Revolver*. Capitol 2576.

————, *Sergeant Pepper's Lonely Hearts Club Band*. Capitol 2653.

————, *The White Album*. Apple 101.

————, *Abbey Road*. Apple SO 383.

————, *1962/66*. Capitol SEBX 11842.

————, *1967/70*. Capitol SEBX 11843.

Rolling Stones, *Rolling Stones*. London PS 375.

————, *Out of Our Heads*. London PS 429.

————, *Aftermath*. London PS 476.

————, *Between the Buttons*. London PS 499.

————, *Their Satanic Majesties Request*. London PS NPS 2.

————, *Beggars Banquet*. London PS 539.

————, *Let it Bleed*. London NPS 4.

————, *Hot Rocks 1964/71*. London PS 606/7.

————, *Some Girls*. Rolling Stones COC 39108.

————, *Emotional Rescue*. Rolling Stones COC 16015.

————, *Rewind 1971-84*. Rolling Stones EJ 2601061.

7

The Times They Are A-Changin': The American Rock Scene, 1964-69

The Beatles invasion and that of other British groups that followed, some great, some forgettable, heralded a new age in American music. It swept away many of the forgettable stars of the early 60s. It also opened a new musical door for young Americans who wanted to express their own musicality. The Beatles proved that rock music could have a message, that it could be more than teenage sighing set to a beat. The American musical scene was ready to respond.

THE FOLK REVIVAL

In the early 60s, American pop music was not dominated entirely by the teen idols and Motown. Another group of musicians had come forward, armed with acoustic guitars, banjos, and songs that carried a message. This was the age of John F. Kennedy, a young president who bore the promise of change. It was a time when civil rights marchers were moving through the South, trying to end the segregation that had kept blacks out of American life for so many years. A prime tool in social change were songs like "We Shall Overcome" and "I Shall Not Be Moved," songs that expressed rebellion as forcefully as the hits of the Rolling Stones (see Chapter 6). The folk singers' message was simple: Music could change the world.

Bob Dylan

A leader in the folk revival who became a key player in rock music was a young Minnesotan born Robert Zimmerman (1941-   ), who renamed himself Bob Dylan in honor of Welsh poet Dylan Thomas. In the mid-50s, he fell in love with black R&B music, and began performing in high school in a rock band. During college, he was exposed to folk music, particularly the work of Woody Guthrie (1912-1967). In 1960, he traveled to New York to seek out his idol.

Guthrie was one of America's great songwriters. He had written such classics as "This Land Is Your Land," "Reuben James," "Do-Re-Mi," and other songs that commented on the plight of America's rural poor during the hard days of the Depression. Although other country singers before Guthrie had written songs with a message, Guthrie was the first to show how a message could be molded into a memorable melody. Guthrie was hardly a great guitarist, and his voice carried the nasal twang of his Oklahoma upbringing. But this, too, was an inspiration to Dylan and countless others, who realized that it wasn't necessary to croon like Bing Crosby to be a pop star.

Dylan met Guthrie, who was hospitalized in New York with an incurable disease, and soon he became the darling of the New York folk world. He recorded two albums for Columbia Records, the second showing that he had fully absorbed the Guthrie style. Two classic songs came from this album, "Blowin' in the Wind" and "Don't Think Twice, It's Alright." The first song commented on social issues, such as nuclear war and the civil rights marches. In the second, more wistful, song Dylan expresses both affection and anger, love and contempt, over an ended love affair. Dylan was already demonstrating his ability to fuse personal protest with broader issues.

1964 brought his third album, and the classic "The Times They Are A-Changin'." Dylan, viewed as a third-rate guitarist and tenth-rate singer by people in the business, was still admired as a songwriter. Folk groups like Peter, Paul, and Mary were scoring hits with his songs, and rock bands were also beginning to cover his material. His song "Mr. Tambourine Man" was the first hit for a new group called the Byrds (see below).

Early 1965 brought Dylan's first major career change. He abandoned folk music to become a full-fledged rock performer. His songs took on a wilder, freer form, and the hard-driving rock accompaniment mirrored their angry energy. His first hit in the rock form was "Like a Rolling Stone," a song that gains momentum as line builds on line, culminating in the triumphant chorus: "How does it feel?"—a question that had great meaning for an entire generation of frustrated, rebellious teenagers.

Dylan was more than a musician. For many college-educated young people he became a kind of prophet. They hung on his every word. Through 1965 and 1966, he continued to deliver strong personal statements in three albums, *Bring It All Back Home*, *Highway 61 Revisited*, and *Blonde on Blonde*. Song after song, each more complex than the last, came from his pen. The songs became mini epics, reaching beyond the rules of the three minute, verse-chorus-verse-chorus form that had dominated previous pop and rock music. Although it was not clear exactly what any one song *meant*, it was clear that Dylan's songs implied more than what they stated. Although these records were not Top-10 hits, they were perhaps the most listened-to songs of any composer in the 60s.

Bob Dylan. Courtesy the artist

Dylan's amazing output came to a sudden end in summer 1966, when he nearly died in a motorcycle accident. A self-imposed exile followed, and the "new" Dylan that emerged in 1967 once again took on a different role, this time as a country balladeer. Through the late 60s, the 70s, and 80s, Dylan has continued to chart a zigzag course through pop music. Although not always successful, he has always challenged the conventions. He is the conscience of pop music, less interested in making hits than in drawing attention to specific issues.

Simon and Garfunkel

Rock and roll is the product of many and varied influences. There is no duo in the history of rock that shows this more strongly than Paul Simon (1942-   ) and Art Garfunkel (1942-   ), who achieved a string of hits in the mid-60s.

The two met in high school in Queens, New York. Both came from middle-class homes; both loved black rock and roll. Influenced by the Everly Brothers, they took the name Tom and Jerry from the popular cartoon about a cat and a mouse. Soon, they had a hit record, "Hey School Girl," which sounded like countless other teen records of the late 50s.

After their brief encounter with success, the two entered college. Simon was influenced by New York-based folk singers. He began composing his own songs and playing the acoustic guitar. Like Dylan, he was equally influenced by poets as by musicians, and also like Dylan, many of his songs commented on contemporary events. Depressed by life in America and his own lack of success, he left for England, soon after recording an album of folk and protest songs for Columbia Records with old pal Garfunkel. It was the summer of 1963, right before the Beatles broke in America.

A DJ heard this first album, and was impressed by one song, a brooding folk ballad called "The Sounds of Silence." The duo had recorded it with a simple, stark guitar accompaniment. This DJ realized that by adding bass and drums, the song could be transformed into the rock style. Without Simon's or Garfunkel's participation, Columbia doctored the song and suddenly they had a Number-1 hit. Simon was called back from England to rejoin Garfunkel to produce an album to capitalize on their sudden success.

The songs that he wrote were every bit as intellectual as his earlier folk compositions. "I Am a Rock, I Am an Island," alludes to the famous line, "No man is an island," from English poet John Donne.

"Richard Cory" took the words of Edward Arlington Robinson, an American poet of the late 19th century, and set them to a rolling rock beat. Simon was breaking all the rules of simple teen lyrics and, surprisingly, he was discovering an audience that was equally atuned to his sophisticated songwriting.

The duo continued to score hits through the 60s, including everything from the lighthearted "Feelin' Groovy" to the anthem-like "Bridge Over Troubled Water." Simon scored the influential movie *The Graduate*, which introduced the ultimate antihero actor, Dustin Hoffman, to the American screen. As solo performers, Simon and Garfunkel continued to work through the 70s, with Simon the more successful of the pair. He continued to write in a highly erudite manner, while drawing on diverse musical styles. Although his popularity ebbed and flowed, he recently returned triumphantly to the American musical scene with the album *Graceland*, combining African musical instruments and melodies with contemporary lyrics.

The Lovin' Spoonful and the Mamas and the Papas

Two groups that came out of the New York City folk scene were the Lovin' Spoonful and the Mamas and the Papas. In fact, the seeds for both bands were laid in 1964 when a group of New York City folk performers came together for a short period to experiment with playing in a rock band. The band was called the Mugwumps; half of its members went on to form the Spoonful, the other half moved to California and formed the Mamas and the Papas.

The Lovin' Spoonful was a band centered on guitarist/harmonica player/songwriter John Sebastian (1944-   ). Sebastian had been active in the New York City folk scene and had written a song, "Younger Girl," which was a hit for a local New York rock band. The Spoonful's sound, called "good-time music" by critics, took elements from the folk tradition to create a highly listenable form of rock and roll. Sebastian's music and lyrics were pleasant and nonthreatening, the exact opposite of the music of the Rolling Stones.

From 1965 to 1967, Sebastian wrote a string of hits—"Do You Believe in Magic?"; "Daydream"; "Rain on the Roof"; "Summer in the City"—which defined the Spoonful's soft-rock sound. One of the band's last great hits, "Younger Generation," defined the trials and tribulations of the generation gap, projecting that the next generation would probably face similar problems with their parents as did the 1960s hippies.

The Mamas and the Papas were formed by former New York folk musician John Phillips (1935-   ), his wife Michelle (1944-   ), singer Cass Elliott (1943-1974), and Canadian folksinger Denny Doherty (1941-   ). The group's sound was defined by their unique vocal harmonies, borrowed from their folk roots. Lush arrangements, drawing as heavily on orchestral instruments as on the basic instruments of rock and roll, were created for the group by their producer/manager Lou Adler.

The group's greatest hits defined the California sound for the mid-60s. These include "California Dreamin'," featuring a jazzy flute solo and the gospel-influenced lead vocal of Phillips, and "Monday, Monday," noteworthy for the innovative use of call-and-response between the lead vocalist and the rest of the group.

The Byrds

One of the first rock groups to be deeply influenced by the Beatles were the Byrds. The group's members came from the folk revival. All were seasoned performers; Jim McGuinn (1942-   ; he later changed his name to Roger), began as a guitarist for teen idol Bobby Darin and folk star Judy Collins before he struck out on his own as a singer/songwriter performing in New York's Greenwich Village. He traveled to Los Angeles where he met another struggling folk musician, David Crosby (1941-   ). In the wake of the success of the Beatles, the two decided to form an electric rock band. The problem was to find other musicians.

They drew on the local folk community. A mandolin player who specialized in bluegrass music named Chris Hillman (1942-   ) was enthralled with the Beatles, too. He joined the group as bass player. Gene Clark (1941-   ), another local singer/songwriter, came along for the ride. The least likely candidate was Michael Clarke (1943-   ), who was convinced by the others to take up the drums, although he had no previous musical experience. They grew long bangs—following John, Paul, Ringo, and George—and even took the preposterous name the Beefeaters to project a proper English heritage. Soon, the name was changed to the Byrds (the odd spelling being an hommage to you-know-who), and the group was off the ground.

Although they were determined to rock, their repertoire was strictly folk. From Pete Seeger came "The Bells of Rhymney" and "Turn, Turn, Turn," and from Dylan "Mr. Tambourine Man." The sound was molded by two key elements. They took the Beatles's idea of harmony and made it even more elaborate, blending four soaring voices where the Beatles had at best three. Next came the chiming sound of McGuinn's electric twelve-string guitar. The twelve-string, well-known in folk circles, was a novelty in rock. When it was electrified, it created a swirling, ringing sound that made the Byrds's music powerfully hypnotic.

The Byrds reached their zenith in 1966, when their music became increasingly complex and spacey. The California spirit of free love, drugs, and rebellion all played into the soft rock of such hits as "Eight Miles High," which is about flying, drug taking, day dreaming, or all of the above. McGuinn's twelve-string solo was breathtaking, and unusually inventive for pop music. He drew his inspiration from the jazz improvisations of saxophonist John Coltrane as much as he did from any rock musician. The song's unearthly harmonies and dense sound made it an anthem for hippies throughout the country.

By 1967, the group was falling apart. Their swansong were two country rock albums, the uneven *Notorious Byrd Brothers* (the group was down to three members by this point) and *Sweetheart of the Rodeo*, the product of a reconstituted membership. Although this album pointed the way for later innovators like the Eagles, the Byrds had already served their purpose in the first years of rock.

THE SAN FRANCISCO SOUND

At the corner of Haight and Ashbury streets, a revolution in life-style—and music—occurred in the California city of San Francisco. In the mid-60s, a group of young college dropouts and recent graduates gravitated to this rundown neighborhood, where housing was inexpensive. They became known as "hippies." Artists, writers, and musicians gravitated to this area where they could meet and interact. Soon people from all over the country were coming to live in this "hippest" of neighborhoods. Bands like Country Joe and the Fish, Moby Grape, Quicksilver Messenger Service, and many, many others formed in this creative atmosphere. Some were short-lived, and were known only locally, while others had a national audience.

The Jefferson Airplane

One of the first great San Francisco bands was the Jefferson Airplane. Its members came from the folk-revival community. Singer Marty Balin (1942-   ) had been popular in clubs in the Bay

Area for several years. He had fronted a folk trio featuring guitarist Paul Kantner and female vocalist Signe Anderson that was similar in style to Peter, Paul, and Mary. The three were blown away by the sound of the Beatles, and like the founding members of the Byrds, decided to form a rock band.

The local scene provided the extra hands necessary to make up the band. A hot young guitarist with the unusual name of Jorma Kaukonen (1940-   ) was enlisted. He was friendly with a wild bass player, named Jack Casady (1944-   ), who sported round, wire-framed sunglasses. The folk community was not a spawning ground for drummers, who were not needed in acoustic groups, so Balin talked another local guitarist into taking up the drums. And thus the group was born.

The Airplane were important because they were the first local band to land a recording contract, with influential RCA records. The first album was a mixture of tentative rock, social protest, and folk. The band was somewhat directionless, with Balin's strong personality overwhelming singer Anderson, whose voice was too sweet-natured for rock and roll. She was soon replaced by vocalist Grace Slick (1939-   ), from the San Francisco band The Great Society.* Slick not only sang in a breathy, energetic, deep voice but also composed unusually compelling songs. The Airplane was ready for take off.

1967 brought their second, and greatest, album, *Surrealistic Pillow*. It contained such classic Slick songs as "White Rabbit," which is about Alice in Wonderland, taking drugs, neither, or both, and "Somebody to Love," a powerful song about the need for love in a country marked by race riots and the shadow of the Vietnam war. The album cover was as much a statement as the music it contained: The group posed with a variety of instruments, as if to reflect the meeting of folk, rock, blues, and jazz that was their music.

Volunteers, their next album, was more directly a political statement, criticizing the policies of the Johnson/Nixon years of American government. American society appeared to be closed to its young, whose creative solutions to the problems of modern life were generally disregarded. The album cover, which parodied a newspaper

---

* This group took its name from Lyndon Johnson's "great society" programs to improve American life. Johnson, who escalated American involvement in the Vietnam war, was a favorite target of San Francisco-based musicians.

Jefferson Airplane. Courtesy RCA
Records

and featured a picture of an open peanut-butter-and-jelly sandwich
on the inside fold, was itself revolutionary, both in its humor and
defiance of the standards of the typical American record album.

The Airplane was a great vocal band, with Balin and Slick singing
striking harmonies. They were also one of the first great instrumental
bands. Kaukonen and Kantner would take lengthy solos; bass player
Casady was more than an accompanist, often stepping into a solo role
just like a jazz performer. Drummer Spencer Dryden (who replaced
the group's original, less-than-competent folk drummer) propelled
the band with unusual rhythms. The band was a product of all of its
parts. The long instrumentals that they performed in concert were
highly influential on other Bay Area outfits.

The Grateful Dead

The best-known and longest-lasting of all San Francisco bands is
the Grateful Dead, founded in 1965 and still going strong today.
Founded by an ex-bluegrass banjo player turned improvisational
guitarist, Jerry Garcia (1942-   ), the band has defined the San
Francisco sound while defying the commercial norms of rock music.

The Grateful Dead are most famous for their stage act, rather than recordings. They specialize in long, improvised solos, sometimes stretching to thirty minutes or more. The band has gone through several musical stages. Their first album, released in 1967, featured rock arrangements of folk and blues standards. This was followed by several albums that emphasized the spacey, improvised nature of the band's work. These albums include *Anthem of the Sun* (1968) and the ultimate record of their stage show, *Live/Dead* (1970).

Their sound mellowed considerably in the early 70s, beginning with *Workingman's Dead*. Suddenly, the songs featured lush vocal harmonies and carefully worked out arrangements, in sharp contrast to their earlier "loose as a goose" style. The influence of folk and country music is strong in these records. Through the 1970s, the Dead combined folk, jazz, and rock influences to produce a variety of records.

The Dead have attracted perhaps the most loyal fans in rock history. Calling themselves "Deadheads," fans of the group have set up newsletters and telephone hotlines to get all the latest information on the group. Tours are rarely widely promoted, yet Dead fans will often travel from city to city to catch every show in a tour. Recently, with the song"Touch of Grey," the band scored their first-ever hit—a testimony to their longevity. Even in the 1980s, Grateful Dead fans wear the requisite faded blue jeans and tie-dyed tee shirts that were the uniform on the 1960s hippies.

Santana

Named for guitarist Carlos Santana (1947-   ), Santana was one of the few multiracial rock bands, comprising black, Latino, and white members. Santana's music was a mix of rock, jazz, and Latin *salsa*. The instrumentation of the group expanded the standard rock lineup, particularly in the percussion department. The standard rock drum kit was augmented by *timbales* and other Latin percussion instruments.

Like the Grateful Dead, Santana specialized in playing long, complicated pieces that focused on the instrumental textures rather than vocals. However, unlike the Dead's rambling, free-for-all style, Santana's arrangements were highly polished and carefully planned. Their music was probably the most painstakingly arranged of any rock ever produced. Santana produced two highly successful albums in 1969 and 1970 before fading from the scene for some time. The band still tours today, although most of the personnel has changed.

Janis Joplin and Big Brother and the Holding Company

One of the greatest female singers to come out of the San Francisco scene was Texas-born Janis Joplin (1943-1970). Joplin began her career as a folk/blues singer. On arriving in San Francisco to join in the growing music scene, Joplin hooked up with a local band of limited musical ability but high energy. The group, Big Brother and the Holding Company, was catapulted to fame by Joplin's powerful singing. It produced the classic album *Cheap Thrills* in 1968 before Joplin left the band to pursue a solo career. In 1970, just as her career was getting under way, Joplin was found dead of an overdose of heroin.

Joplin was an incredibly gifted singer who had a strong impact on her audience. She sang the blues with an intensity that showed how deeply she felt each song. Unlike other white singers who imitated the black blues style, Joplin absorbed the quality of the blues as well as the sound. Joplin's raspy voice ranged from a begging whisper to a defiant scream. She took blues standards like "Ball and Chain" and "Piece of My Heart" and transformed them into personal statements about the pain that she felt as a woman living in a male-dominated world.

Her flamboyant stage manner—and her private life, including lesbian affairs and heavy drug use—added to her mystique. Joplin became a key figure, particularly for women of her generation, who were amazed by the freedom and power that she seemed to embody. Although her life ended tragically, the legacy of her music and performances lives on in groups like Heart and performers like Joan Jett.

Jimi Hendrix

Jimi Hendrix (1942-1970) is the last great West Coast musician of the era, and perhaps the ultimate "flower child" of the 60s. Born in Seattle, Hendrix began his career as a backup guitarist, playing for Little Richard (see Chapter 3) and other soul artists. In the mid-60s, he formed his first goup, Jimmy James and the Blue Flames, playing blues standards for audiences in Greenwich Village. On hearing Bob Dylan, Hendrix decided that he could be a vocalist. In late 1966, Hendrix moved to England and formed his power trio, The Jimi Hendrix Experience. The group returned to the United States to play at the Monterey Pop Festival in California in 1967, the same festival that propelled Janis Joplin and the Jefferson Airplane to wider fame.

Hendrix was an exceptionally gifted, innovative guitarist, specializing in effects achieved through distortion and super-loud amplification. His first hit album, *Are You Experienced?*, introduced the sound, particularly in the classic song "Purple Haze." The group's first album was perhaps their best. On it, the basic sound of drums, bass, and guitar was used most strongly. The driving drum beat and intricate bass riffs formed the basic layers onto which was added Hendrix's amazing guitar playing. Unlike other guitarists who achieved distorted effects and fuzz tones seemingly by chance, Hendrix learned how to control and use distortion exactly as he wanted. He was able to create a fuzzy, distorted tone on two or three strings while playing clearly on the remaining strings, creating the effect of two guitars playing at once. He could play loudly and melodically at the same time.

Like Joplin, Hendrix was as important a person as performer. In his performances there was a powerful sense of rebelliousness that spoke to the young people of the era. He was one of the first black performers to appeal primarily to the white market. But he made no concessions in style, dress, or personality; he was not a sanitized performer, to say the least! He would occasionally destroy his guitar on stage after his performance. Hendrix, like Joplin, died tragically of a drug overdose. His records continue to sell strongly nearly twenty years after his death, and his influence is evident in the playing of all guitarists.

READ

Cott, Jonathan, *Dylan*. NY: Doubleday, 1984.

Dalton, David, *Piece of My Heart: The Life, Time, and Legend of Janis Joplin*. NY: St. Martins, 1986.

Dylan, Bob, *Writings and Drawings*. NY: Knopf, 1975.

Flanagan, Bill, *Written in My Soul: Rock's Great Songwriters*. NY: Contemporary Books, 1986.

Gans, David, and Peter Simon, *Playing in the Band*. NY: St. Martins, 1985.

Guthrie, Woody, *Bound for Glory*. NY: E. P. Dutton, 1968.

Hampton, Wayne, *Guerilla Minstrels: John Lennon, Joe Hill, Woody Guthrie, and Bob Dylan*. University of Tennessee, 1986.

Hopkins, Jerry, *Hit and Run: The Jimi Hendrix Story*. NY: Putnam, 1983.

Humphries, Patrick, *Bookends: The Simon and Garfunkel Story*. NY: Proteus, 1983.

Jackson, Blair, *The Grateful Dead*. NY: Delilah Books, 1983.

McDonagh, Jack, *San Francisco Rock*. San Francisco, CA: Chronicle Books, 1985.

Scaduto, Anthony, *Dylan*. NY: Grosset & Dunlap, 1971.

Shelton, Robert, *No Direction Home*. NY: Morrow, 1986.

LISTEN

Big Brother and the Holding Company, *Cheap Thrills*. Columbia 9700.

Byrds, *Mr. Tambourine Man*. Columbia 9172.

————, *Younger than Yesterday*. Columbia 9442.

————, *Sweetheart of the Rodeo*. Columbia 9670.

Dylan, Bob, *Bob Dylan*. Columbia 1779.

————, *Times They Are A-Changin'*. Columbia 2105.

————, *Blonde on Blonde*. Columbia C2S 281.

————, *Greatest Hits*. Columbia 2663.

————, *Greatest Hits Volume 2*. Columbia 31120.

Grateful Dead, *Grateful Dead*. Warner Brothers 1689.

————, *Live/Dead*. Warner Brothers 1830.

————, *Workingman's Dead*. Warner Brothers 1869.

Great Society, *Conspicuous Only in its Absence*. Columbia 9624.

Hendrix, Jimi, *Are You Experienced?* Reprise RS 6261.

————, *Smash Hits*. Reprise MS 2025.

Jefferson Airplane, *Surrealistic Pillow*. RCA LSP 3766.

————, *Volunteers*. RCA LSP 4238.

Joplin, Janis, *Pearl*. Columbia 30322.

Lovin' Spoonful, *Do You Believe in Magic?* Kama Sutra 8050.

————, *Best of Vol. 1*. Kama Sutra 2608.

Mamas and the Papas, *If You Can Believe Your Eyes and Ears*. Dunhill 50006.

————, *Farewell to the First Golden Era*. Dunhill 50025.

Santana, *Abraxas*. Columbia 30130.

————, *Greatest Hits*. Columbia 33050.

Simon and Garfunkel, *The Sound of Silence*. Columbia 9049.

————, *Greatest Hits*. Columbia 31350.

8

The Super Groups

To the history of rock and roll, some groups have contributed important music, in the form of new types of songs, innovative lyrics, different instrumentation, or even new styles of dressing or dancing. These groups certainly are important. But there are other groups that have achieved a mythical status. They have contributed to the history of culture as well as the history of music. We've already highlighted some of these groups and individuals: the Beatles, the Rolling Stones, the Supremes, Bob Dylan, and Janis Joplin, to name a few.

The groups discussed in this chapter achieved their greatest popularity—and created their best music— toward the end of the 1960s, just as the rock era was reaching maturity. They were called "supergroups" because they featured the best musicians, whose songs surpassed all that came before. Although some lasted only briefly and others struggled bravely on, all are remembered today for their musical achievement.

THE KIDS ARE ALRIGHT: THE WHO

The Who was one of rock's longest-lasting bands, starting in 1963 and not officially disbanding until the mid-80s. Although their story shares some similarities with the Beatles's and the Stones's, this group has had a unique impact on the history of rock and has also effected social changes in England and the United States.

Like the Stones, the Who began their life as an R&B-influenced band. They performed cover versions of black American songs of the 50s and early 60s. Also like the Stones, the Who were not picture-pretty teen idols. In fact, the first publicity shots of the band suggest a group of outcasts from the high school dance.

Dominating the image was lead guitarist/songwriter Pete Townsend (1945-   ), perhaps the least attractive rock idol ever. His large nose, craggy face, and angry eyes expressed contempt for anyone foolish enough to question his music. Lead singer Roger Daltry (1944-   ) looked like an escapee from reform school, although with his blond hair and expressive face he could take on a more conventional appearance. The two other band members hardly added sex appeal: Bassist John Entwistle (1944-   ) was pudgy and sullen and barely uttered a word on stage. Round-faced and droopy-eyed drummer Keith Moon (1947-1978) flailed away at his drum kit with barely controlled energy.

From the start, the Who were more than a band; they made a political statement. Their first manager cleverly recognized a new social fashion movement in England, which had gained the nickname "mod." The mods were on the cutting edge of fashion, wearing tight-fitting, high-style clothing, popping pep pills to add to their manic energy, and listening to American R&B. The Who's manager renamed the group the High Numbers, and chose songs with titles like "I'm the Face" to align them with the mod movement. This was in spite of the fact that three of the four group members came from a lower-class London neighborhood, and none of them were particularly fashion conscious or good looking.

The group was fortunate to quickly find more competent management in the team of Kit Lambert and Chris Stamp. Lambert and Stamp were key movers and shakers in the growing mod movement, in touch with artists and writers as well as rockers. They built on the Who's high-energy, angry performance style and honed it to perfection. It was their idea for the band to destroy its instruments at the end of every performance, beginning with Townsend madly thrashing his guitar in frustration and culminating in Moon kicking apart his drum set. This expression of rage and defiance was probably as important as the music that preceded it.

The band's first hit was 1965's "My Generation," which, like the Rolling Stones's "Satisfaction," put them on the map. The lyrics, music, and sound of the song came together in a near perfect match. The awkwardness of the group, reflecting every teen's difficulty at self-expression, is underscored by Daltrey's exaggerated, stuttering delivery of the lyrics:

People try to put us d-d-down
Just because we g-g-get around

Things they do look awful c-c-cold
Hope I die before I get old

Although he struggles to get his point across, he spits the words
out in angry triumph when he reveals that he'd rather be dead than be
a part of his parents' world.

From the first, the Who managed to attract two different
audiences. On one hand, as brash kids who sang nasty songs and
smashed their instruments, they appealed to those teens who felt like
outcasts and had difficulty expressing their anger and frustration. On
the other hand, because their lyrics were more interesting and
thoughtful, the Who quickly developed a following among college-
educated Londoners. Their constant instrument bashing became
something of a joke, and their stage mannerisms—Daltrey swung his
microphone on the end of its cord; Townsend took enormous, exaggerated arm swings before striking a chord; Moon wildly tossed his
drum sticks into the air—parodied the conventions of rock. The Who
was both anti-intellectual and witty at the same time. No band had
ever managed to be both successfully before.

By their second album, the Who were beginning to attain new
levels of sophistication. Kit Lambert, who now served as the group's
producer in the studio as well as its manager, discovered that the

The Who. Courtesy Frank Driggs
Collection

album was ten minutes too short and asked Townsend to fill the gap with a single song. Townsend was baffled, since rock songs traditionally are only three minutes long. He deftly strung together a number of half-finished songs, made up an absurd story line, and titled the whole thing a "mini opera." The result, titled "A Quick One [While He's Away]," established the Who as an avant garde band.

Their following record, *The Who Sell Out* featured classic songs like the hit "I Can See for Miles." The album was conceived as a complete work, rather than just as a collection of songs. It parodied English rock radio stations, including mock ads for underarm deodorant (called "Odorono"), the church, and baked beans. While the parodies pointed up how advertisers use adolescent fantasies and fears to sell their products, the songs themselves commented on these adolescent problems. For example, in "Tattoo" the singer recounts:

Me and my brother were talking to each other
'Bout what makes a man a man,
Is it brains or brawn or the date that he is born on
We just couldn't understand.
Tattoo . . .

The narrator seeks in a symbol, the tattoo, the manhood that he can't achieve on his own.

The Who's greatest accomplishment was 1969's three-album opera, *Tommy*. Townsend was inspired by an old blues song, "Eyesight for the Blind," in creating his story about a blind, pin-ball playing teenager who becomes the leader of his generation. Although the story is uneven, the songs that came out of it are impressive, both for the array of styles and the variety of sounds that a four-piece band was able to achieve. Classics like "Pinball Wizard," "Acid Queen," and "See Me" stand out from the rest, but it is remarkable that in this collection of 30-plus songs there are very few outright duds. Townsend cleverly uses several melodic and lyric themes throughout the work to draw it together. These refrains, including "See me, feel me, touch me, heal me," take on new meaning as the story progresses.

Tommy showed recording executives that there could be a strong market for a serious three-record rock album. Groups no longer would be tied down to producing hit singles and then coming out with albums to help further promote their hits. Now, they could approach the album as an integral work of art.

Tommy also had a large social impact. The Who came to the United States on several tours from 1967 to 1969, appearing at important festivals like Monterey Pop in California in 1967 and the famous Woodstock festival in 1969 (see Postscript). The message of *Tommy* had many interpretations. Some thought the opera was a reaction against authority; when Tommy becomes a leader, he begins to turn into a despot. Others thought it meant that love could heal any affliction, even blindness. Others thought that *Tommy* was the story of how teenagers, no matter how downtrodden, could lead and change the world. Whatever the interpretation, the message of *Tommy* inspired the hippie movement in the United States, with its belief in free love and antiwar, antiestablishment philosophies.

The Who lived in the shadow of *Tommy* for many years. Although they sought to recapture their role as merely a fun-loving rock and roll band, they were expected to continue to produce monumental works. The burden fell particularly heavily on songwriter Townsend, who didn't necessarily envision himself as a rock and roll Verdi. The problems were complicated by Daltrey's transformation from rough kid into actor and teen idol in the 70s. While Daltrey sang the songs, he couldn't write them; Townsend, with limited vocal abilities, couldn't sing but was an excellent writer. The tension between the two was bound to be enormous because each felt that he was the star of the band.

The Who's legacy is important musically, lyrically, and politically. Musically, they set the stage for all the powerful bands that followed, particularly heavy metal bands that rely on physical acrobatics when performing. Lyrically, Townsend showed that rock composers could write more thoughtfully, raising issues that would reflect the darker side of teenage life, such as jealousy, insecurity, fear, and violence. Politically, the Who showed how a band could inspire a generation without preaching to them.

POWER TRIO: CREAM

For a period in the mid-60s, you could see scrawled on many a wall in London's club district the legend: "Clapton is God." The young guitar player to whom this referred was Eric Clapton (1945-   ), one of England's greatest musicians. Like many other guitar players, he began his career playing the blues, copying the styles of Americans Muddy Waters, B. B. King, and the Chicago bluesmen (see Chapter 1). His work with the Yardbirds and John Mayall's Bluesbreakers reveals these blues influences, and it helped to bring new prominence to the originators of the blues sound in America and Britain.

Clapton's greatest fame came during a brief period between 1966 and 1968 when he formed the unconventional rock trio, Cream. Along with bassist Jack Bruce (1943-) and drummer Ginger Baker (1939-), Clapton's goal was to form a group that would highlight the improvisational skills of the musicians. He was influenced by small American jazz bands in choosing to emphasize instrumental dexterity over lyrics and improvisation over planning. However, the style of the band was rooted in rock and blues, not jazz. In the words of rock critic Dave Marsh, "Cream created the fastest, loudest, most overpowering blues-based rock ever heard, particularly on stage."

Cream's recordings, particularly their second album, *Disraeli Gears* (1967), were influential, but it was their stage show that really set the rock world on fire. Clapton was an awesome guitar player, who could effortlessly spin out riffs and complex melodic lines while producing a flawless, singing tone. Baker was an energetic drummer, who went beyond the four-square rhythms and predictable patterns of ordinary rock. Without a rhythym guitarist, Bruce's role became crucial to holding the band together, and to complementing Clapton's lead parts with his own work. His bass work went far beyond the average rock playing. Bruce was a consummate musician who could match Clapton's considerable skills.

The band dissolved, leaving Clapton to go through a series of bands and, later on, solo work. By the mid-70s, drug addiction temporarily halted his career. Of late, he has returned to playing, and his albums have met with success. Clapton's blues-based guitar work, prominently featured on stage although (sadly) less prominently on his recordings, is still among rock's finest.

THE DOORS

One of the groups of the late 60s that has had the most lasting influence on rock history came out of Southern California. The group was neither particularly talented as a rock outfit nor were its songs particularly original. It had two things going for it, however; the unusually talented keyboard player Ray Manzarek, whose swirling organ playing set new standards for the instrument in rock, and vocalist Jim Morrison (1943-1971), whose performance style laid the basis for Alice Cooper, David Lee Roth, and countless others.

The band began playing together in 1966 at the popular L.A. club, Whiskey A Go Go. The Doors was noteworthy for Morrison's commanding presence and shouting vocal style and its improvisational instrumental work. The band's first album, *The Doors* (1967), included its biggest hit, "Light My Fire." This song was unusual because it featured a long, improvised instrumental part that was omitted from the single. However, the longer version became a favorite on FM radio, which was not as limited in its format as Top-40 (AM) stations. The suggestive lyrics made it slightly risky for Top-40 stations to play it at all, and Morrison's sly vocal delivery did the most to underscore the sexual connotation of every word:

> You know that I would be untrue,
> You know that I would be a liar,
> If I were to say to you,
> Girl we couldn't get much higher.
> Chorus:
> Come on baby light my fire,
> Come on baby light my fire,
> Try to set the night on . . . fire!

This initial hit was followed by a string of hit singles. Although the songs were not particularly original, they did manage to capture the eery, alienated feeling of many teens. Morrison's "People Are Strange" captured the feeling of being an outcast in its gloomy lyrics:

> People are strange, when you're a stranger
> Faces look ugly when you're alone . . .
> Chorus:
> When you're strange,
> Faces come out of the rain,
> When you're strange,
> No one remembers your name,
> When you're strange, when you're strange,
> when you're strange. All right now.

Other songs vaguely commented on social issues, including the anti-war song "The Unknown Soldier," and Morrison's plea for free love, "Hello, I Love You." Although not all of these songs were particularly noteworthy lyrically or melodically, the strength of Morrison's vocals, and the band's ability to hammer home a simple melodic riff, made them memorable.

Jim Morrison of the Doors.
Courtesy Elektra Records

Morrison's stage antics became more and more outrageous as his dependence on alcohol and drugs increased. He was jailed in 1969 for indecent exposure during a Miami concert. Although this behavior was supposedly revolutionary because it challenged contemporary morals, it was more often pathetic. Morrison would forget the words to his songs, stagger drunkenly, and look out in a daze on the audience as he tried to win their love. The need to be outrageous took over any attempt at performing.

The band's albums of the period 1969-70 reflected Morrison's deterioration. The Doors attempted to broaden their musical style on *The Soft Parade* by including brass and strings, but they were not accomplished enough musically to make any use of these additions. Morrison, meanwhile, began to fancy that he was a poet, and his lyrics became self-consciously "literary." He even recorded some "songs" in 1971 which featured him reciting his poetry to the band's improvised backup.

In mid-1971, Morrison left the group to travel to Paris to live as an expatriot literary figure. He undoubtedly imagined that the world that authors Ernest Hemingway and Gertrude Stein described in the 1920s still existed there. Instead, he began drinking heavily again, and died of a heart attack while taking a bath.

To⠀

The amazing thing about Morrison and his music is that the Doors's recordings still sell strongly today. Although the group's later work is mostly forgotten, the records made between 1967-69 hold a strong attraction for the rock audience. Morrison's death at age 27 elevated him to the level of a cult figure. He is remembered not so much for the facts of his life as for the image that he created: the revolutionary, powerful singer who challenged society's rigid code of behavior.

THE BAND

The Band was part of "The Woodstock generation," a group of counterculture artists and musicians who chose to live in and around Woodstock, New York. This tiny town in the Catskill Mountains had been a haven for artists since the turn of the century. The town is near enough to New York City for artists to take care of their business concerns there, while still offering the joys of country life. Bob Dylan settled in Woodstock after his motorcycle accident in 1966, along with his manager, Albert Grossman, and members of his backup group, who would soon be known as "The Band."

The Band leapt onto the American music scene with the release of their first album *Music from Big Pink* (1968), conceived in their large pink house outside of Woodstock. For all anyone knew, they were newcomers to the rock scene. However, by the time this album was released, they were veterans of years of touring.

The group originated in Arkansas, centering around drummer/vocalist Levon Helm (1942-   ). They traveled to Canada as the backup group for Ronnie Hawkins, a country-rock singer who found in the early 60s that the audience for his music was stronger up north than in his native country. The group took the name "the Hawks" and soon were crisscrossing Canada with Hawkins. By the mid-60s, even Hawkins's Canadian reputation was declining, so the band struck out on their own.

The instrumental lineup of the group was unique. Helms, as drummer and leader, held the group together with his powerful, staccato bursts of drumbeats and his down-home country vocal delivery. The shy guitarist (Jaime) Robbie Robertson (1944-   ) was a first-rate rock player, with a strong blues influence in his lead work. Most unusual was the incorporation of two keyboard players, pianist Richard Manuel (1945-1986) and organist Garth Hudson

HAVERSTRAW
KINGS DAUGHTERS
PUBLIC LIBRARY
THIELLS BRANCH
1 ROSMAN ROAD
GARNERVILLE, N.Y 10923

The Band. Courtesy Frank Driggs Collection

(1943-   ), whose style showed the influence of gospel, jazz, and blues. Bassist Rick Danko (1943-   ) finished the lineup, whose work showed the influence of Motown as well as country.

The Band was not tied down to this instrumental format; in fact, they were as comfortable playing acoustic as electric, and you could hear mandolin, accordion, and acoustic guitar in their work. Unlike other bands that centered on one vocalist, everyone except Robertson and Hudson sang, and the harmonies and vocal quality that they produced was definitely country in origin.

Through blues guitarist John Hammond Jr. (son of the famous record producer), the Hawks were introduced to New York audiences in 1964. In 1965-66, they joined Bob Dylan as his backup group (although Dylan replaced Helms with another drummer, perhaps trying to assert his authority over the ensemble). They then retired with Dylan to the Catskills after his accident, and began writing songs and recording a massive amount of demo tapes, later released in the 70s as the "Basement Tapes."

In 1968, their creative experiments bore fruit in their first album. The album defied rock traditions. The cover was a painting by Bob Dylan showing the band at work. The back cover showed a picture of Big Pink, the house that inspired the music. On the inside jacket, the members of the band posed with their relatives. Nowhere on the record jacket was the name of the group given, except on the record's spine. It was unclear whether "The Band" was their name, or whether it was just a generic name for the group.

The songs on the record were equally unusual; half folk, half gospel, half blues, and half rock, they fused several traditions into their own sound. Songs like "The Weight" had a timeless quality of country gospel. But the words to the song were difficult to understand, even though they *seemed* to mean more than what they said. The chorus is typical:

> Take the load off, Fannie,
> Take the load for free,
> Take the load off Fannie,
> And, and you put the load (put the load) right on me.

The vocal sound was equally unusual. The high falsetto harmonies, the nasal lead vocals, the ragged-edged harmonies, suggested a group of backwoodsmen who had somehow stumbled onto the traditions of Jerry Lee Lewis and Elvis Presley. The instrumental work emphasized the ensemble, in an attempt to create a total sound, rather than highlighting any one soloist.

The group's second album, simply titled *The Band* (1969), was even more firmly rooted in American musical traditions than their first. This was their most successful record in terms of both songs and overall sound. It included the classic "The Night They Drove Old Dixie Down," a song that not only tells a Civil War story but also evokes the sound of that period. The cover photos underscored this 19th-century image, showing band members dressed like pioneer settlers.

After this initial success, the group tried in vain to recapture its earlier vision through a series of less-than-successful albums and on tours on their own and with Dylan. Finally, on Thanksgiving Day 1976 they threw themselves a massive farewell party, joined by friends Dylan, Joni Mitchell, Eric Clapton, Muddy Waters, Neil Young, Ronnie Hawkins, and a number of other members of rock royalty. The entire affair was captured on film by Martin Scorcese. "The Last Waltz," as the concert was called, signaled the end of an era not only for The Band but for many of the performers who appeared with them.[*]

---

[*] Recently, guitarist/songwriter Robbie Robertson has emerged from years of seclusion with a new solo album. The other members of The Band had been touring without him, until the death of Richard Manuel in 1986 cut short their tour.

READ

Butler, Douglas, et al., *Full Moon*. NY: Morrow, 1981.

Hopkins, Jerry, and David Sugerman, *No One Here Gets Out Alive*. NY: Warner Books, 1980.

Spitz, Robert S., *Barefoot in Babylon*. NY: Viking, 1979.

Stein, Jeff and Chris Johnston, *The Who*. NY: Stein and Day, 1983.

LISTEN

Band, *Music from Big Pink*. Capitol ST 2955.

————, *The Band*. Capitol EST 132.

————, *Last Waltz*. Warner Brothers 3WS3146.

Cream, *Fresh Cream*. Atco 33206.

————, *Disraeli Gears*. Atco 33232.

Doors, *Doors*. Elektra 74007.

————, *Waiting for the Sun*. Elektra 74024.

————, *Greatest Hits*. Elektra 515.

Who, *My Generation*. Decca 74664.

————, *Who Sell Out*. Decca 74950.

————, *Tommy*. Decca 7205.

Postscript: Woodstock

There were many rock festivals in the late 60s, including the influential Monterey, California, pop festival of 1967 that introduced Janis Joplin, the Who, and the Jefferson Airplane to a larger audience. But none was more important than 1969's Woodstock, generally viewed as the swansong of the hippie generation.

In the summer of 1969, a group of young promoters decided to throw the ultimate rock party. Originally, they had hoped to find a site in the town of Woodstock, New York, the home of Bob Dylan, which was an artists' community that they thought might welcome a few thousand teenagers on a summer's weekend. However, they had to settle on a farm site outside of town, and began to line up the greatest rock roster that they could muster. Performers at the festival included the Jefferson Airplane, the Who, Joe Cocker, Crosby, Stills, and Nash, John Sebastian (of the Lovin' Spoonful), Arlo Guthrie, and many others. But the true star was the crowd, an unexpectedly large gathering of America's younger generation.

While the promoters thought that they might attract 10- or 20,000 people, the final count of those who showed up on what turned out to be a wet, rainy weekend was over 300,000. There were massive traffic jams on the New York Thruway leading to the event; flood, water, health facilities, and toilets were overburdened by the enormous turnout; 100,000 or so of the crowd didn't even buy tickets—the onslaught of people was simply too difficult to control at the gates.

However, despite the bad weather, massive crowd, and poor facilities, the attendees behaved well. The concert became a massive "love-in"; people shared music, food, liquor, and drugs. They bathed together in the local creek and no violence was reported. The "Woodstock nation" showed the rest of the country how young people could behave.

It is impossible to describe the impact of the festival on those who attended, and also to the millions who watched the event as a movie or heard it as a three-record set. Yet the feelings of artistic and personal freedom that the festival inspired could never be recreated; a few short months later came the famous rock concert at Altamount, California, sponsored by the Rolling Stones that also attracted some 300,000 fans. This event ended tragically, however, when members of the Hell's Angels motorcycle gang viciously attacked members of the crowd.

The rock and roll years of 1955 to 1969 in the United States brought new standards to popular music. Lyrically, melodically, and instrumentally, rock music was far more complex and interesting than the pop music that had preceded it. Although there was a good deal of commercial music of inferior quality that was produced, overall it was a time of great strides in American popular music. It is difficult to imagine that this great creativity can ever be duplicated. Luckily, the legacy of these years lives on in the recordings that these artists made.

Glossary

American Bandstand: This television show, originating in 1956 in Philadelphia, was an important showcase for rock and roll performers through the 1960s. Its host, Dick Clark, became a symbol of rock for American teens. The show is still aired today.

bass guitar: An electrified version of the four-string, upright bass that is played in the symphony orchestra. The bass provides the low accompaniment in the rock combo. Electric bass guitars were introduced by American guitar makers in the mid-1950s and became common in rock bands in the early 60s.

Beatles haircut: A hairstyle pioneered by the Beatles featuring long bangs combed over the forehead. This hairstyle is also described as a "mop top."

Blues growler: The shouting, raspy style of blues singing that conveys deep intensity of feeling.

boogie woogie: A jazz piano style that features a "walking bass," or broken chords played by the left hand.

bridge: The section of a song that links the *chorus* to the *verses.* Often, this part will be in a different key and will feature a different *melody.*

Brill Building: A building in New York City that was the home to many famous music-publishing operations. The songs that were published there were collectively known as "Brill Building pop."

California sound: The light-hearted, good-times sound of groups, such as the Beach Boys, that originated in California.

call and response: A song structure originating in folk music that is often used in rock. In this style, a lead vocalist sings one line or verse (the "call"), and the group "responds" with another phrase, line, or verse.

choke: Holding the left or fretting hand of the guitar over the strings so that no musical sound is produced while strumming vigorously with the right hand. The result is a sharp, staccato sound.

chorus: The repeated part of the lyrics of a song, usually occurring between the *verses*.

chord: A group of three or more notes played at the same time. The common three-note chord is called a *triad*.

cover artist: A performer who "covers" or performs another artist's song. During the period from 1955 to 1970, a cover artists usually was a white performer who sang a song originated by a black artist.

crossover: An artist who is known for one style of music, such as country, is said to "crossover" if he or she has a hit in another style of music, such as rock.

Deadhead: A fan of the San Francisco band, the Grateful Dead.

distortion: A technique used by electric guitarists to create a fuzzy, grainy sound. This sound is created by overloading the amplifier and speakers of the guitar. Also called "fuzz tone."

DJ: The DJ or disc jockey plays records at a rock radio station. The DJ also comments on the music, and, in the early days of rock radio, selected the records to play.

doo wop: A vocal style that imitates the sound of musical instruments. Doo wop groups usually feature the full range of vocalists, from deep bass to high tenor. Doo wop songs often feature nonsense syllables that are sung to imitate instrumental sounds.

duck tail: A hairstyle popularized by Elvis Presley that features an upturned or flipped back curl.

electric blues: A style of blues performance popularized in Chicago. Electric blues usually features a small combo of guitar, piano, harmonica, drums, and occasionally horns. The songs focus on topics centering on the trials and tribulations of love, marriage, holding a job, and life in the big city. Also called "urban blues."

falsetto: Singing in an unnaturally high voice, above the normal vocal range.

feedback: Feedback is created by the electrical interference of the pickup in an electric guitar and its amplifier. The result is a high-pitched, squealing sound.

folk revival: A movement in the early 1960s, led by singer Bob Dylan, that saw the reemergence of folk music in America.

fuzz tone. See *distortion*.

girl group: Popular singing groups of the early 60s that featured teenage girls as vocalists were collectively called the "girl groups." The most famous was the Ronettes.

gospel: A style of religious music, popularized in black churches, that features intensely felt, nearly shouted vocals and a slow-moving, introspective instrumental accompaniment.

Greenwich Village: A New York neighborhood with a bohemian past that became the center of youth culture in New York in the 60s. It was an important area for guitar players, folk singers, and fledgling rock and roll bands.

Haight/Ashbury: A crossroads in San Francisco that was a mecca for teenagers in search of inexpensive housing and companionship in the late 1960s.

happening: A free-form, artistic event usually centering on a musical, theatrical, or dance performance.

harmonica: A small, free-reed instrument, known in blues circles as a "harp."

hippie: General name given to teenagers in the late 1960s who championed free love, world peace, and other liberal causes. Hippies usually had long hair and wore blue jeans or tie-dyed clothing. A large group of hippies lived in the *Haight/Ashbury* section of San Francisco.

honky tonk music: Country music performed in small bars (called "honky tonks") in the Southwest.

improvisation: Creating a melody, lyric, or harmony part based on a general structure, but without any specific preplanned ideas.

jump: A style of jazz born in the late 30s and early 40s that featured upbeat, lighthearted tempi and lyrics. A famous jump star was vocalist/saxophonist Louis Jordan.

lick: A short melodic phrase played by a guitarist. Also called a "riff."

lyric: The words or vocal part of a song.

mellow: A vocal or melodic style that emphasizes soft, easy-to-listen-to sounds. All of the sharp edges or exaggerated feelings are toned down.

melody: The musical line or series of notes that makes up the backbone of a song.

mix: In the recording studio, different "tracks" or parts of the recording are "mixed" together to form a finished product. See *multi-tracking*.

Motown: Motown, derived from "Motor City," Detroit's nickname, was Berry Gordy's fledgling record company in the early 1960s. The word "Motown" has come to mean any highly polished, commercial black music.

multi-tracking: In the recording studio, multi-tracking or "overdubbing" is used to make a more complex end-product than could be achieved by simply recording the musicians "live." For example, a guitarist might play one part and then another part could be recorded later and "overdubbed" onto the original recording. Also called "overtracking."

package show: A special performance put together by a booking agent that highlights several groups performing in a similar style. A common package show would be a "50s revue," featuring bands that were famous in the 50s.

polyrhythm: More than one rhythmic part played at the same time. This style is common in African traditional music, and is extensively used by performers like James Brown.

ragtime: A jazz piano style of the early 20th century that features a steady bass part with a syncopated melody line.

rhythm and blues: The general term given by white record producers and radio station owners to the black music of the late 1940s and early 1950s.

riff. See *lick*.

rock-opera: An extended series of rock songs linked together by a common story. The most famous rock-opera is Pete Townsend's *Tommy*.

rockabilly: A country music style, originated in the 1950s, that combines a rock beat with country subjects.

San Francisco Sound: The style of rock music popularized in San Francisco in the late 1960s by bands like the Jefferson Airplane and Grateful Dead.

singer/songwriter: A performer who plays his own songs. Singer/songwriters would include Bob Dylan and James Taylor.

skiffle: The British name for folk songs performed in a jazzy, uptemp style. The most famous skiffle star was Lonnie Donegan.

soul: The name given to black popular music performed with an intensity usually reserved for *gospel* music.

stanza. See *verse*.

surf music. See *California sound*.

sustain: The ability of an electrified instrument to continue producing a sound long after it is originally played.

swing: Big Band jazz that is performed in a lively, uptempo style to inspire dancing.

synthesizer: An electronic musical instrument that simulates or synthesizes musical sounds.

teen idol: A performer groomed to appeal to teenagers.

texture: The total sound of a song, created by the vocalist, instrumental parts, and any other sounds introduced in the recording process.

timbales: Latin percussion instruments (drums) used by groups like Santana.

twangy guitar: A nasal, tenor sound created by electric guitarist Duane Eddy.

twist: Popular dance of the early 60s introduced by Chubby Checker, featuring rhythmic twisting of the hips.

verse: The nonrepeated portion of a song, usually structured in four-line "stanzas." The verse is alternated with a *chorus*, or repeated part. Sometimes a *bridge* comes between verse and chorus.

wall of sound: A style of recording created by producer Phil Spector that uses many musicians playing the same instruments (ten guitarists and four drummers, for instance) to create a dense sound.

western swing: A musical style that weds country music and jazz.

Woodstock: The location of a 1969 rock festival that was the last great assembly of youth and famous rock bands of the 60s.

Index

A

Aldon music, 37-39
Allison, Jerry, 34
Altamount Racetrack concert, 73
American Bandstand, 43
Are You Experienced, 88
Avalon, Frankie, 43

B

Baker, Ginger, 96
Balin, Marty, 83-84
Band, The, 99-101
Band, The, 101
Bartholomew, Dave, 19
Basement Tapes, 100
Basie, William "Count," 5
Beach Boys, 46-48
Beatles, The, 33, 63-70
Berry, Charles Edward Anderson "Chuck," 20
Best, Pete, 64
Big Brother and the Holding Company, 87
Blake, Eubie, 4
Boogie woogie, 4, 5
Booker T. and the MGs, 58
Boone, Pat, 42
Brill Building sound, 38
Brown, James, 58
Bruce, Jack, 96
Bullock, Anna Mae. *See* Turner, Tina
Burnett, Chester Arthur. *See* Howlin' Wolf

Byrds, The, 82-82

C

Call and response, 1
Casady, Jack, 84
Cavern Club, The, 65
Charles, Ray, 49-51
Checker, Chubby, 43
Chicago blues. *See* Electric blues
Christian, Charley, 3-4
Clapton, Eric, 95-96
Clark, Dick, 43
Clark, Gene, 82
Clarke, Michael, 82
Coasters, The, 17
Cooke, Sam, 51
Cousin Brucey (Bruce Morrow), 15
Cover artists, 41-42
Cream, 95-96
Crickets, The, 34-35
Crosby, David, 82
Crossover music, 45

D

Daltry, Roger, 92, 93, 94, 95
Danko, Rick, 100
Disraeli Gears, 96
Distortion, 3
Doherty, Denny, 82
Domino, Antoine "Fats," 18-19
Doo wop, 15-18
Doors, The, 96-99
Dozier, Lamont, 53

111

Drifters, The, 16-17
Duncan, Tommy, 9-10
Dylan, Bob, 78-80, 99, 100, 103

E-F

Ed Sullivan Show, The, 67
Eddy, Duane, 45-46
Electric blues, 6-9
Elliott, Cass, 82
Entwistle, John, 92
Epstein, Brian, 65-66, 67
Everly Brothers (Phil and Don),
   The, 44-45

Feedback, 3
Folk music, black, 1
Folk revival, 77-83
Four Tops, 53-54
Franklin, Aretha, 58-59
Freed, Alan, 14
Funicello, Annette, 43

G

Garcia, Jerry, 85-86
Garfunkel, Art, 80-81
Gaye, Marvin, 56
Gladys Knight and the Pips, 56
Goffin, Gerry, 38
Good-time music, 81
Gordy, Berry, 52
Grateful Dead, The, 85-86
Great Society, The, 84
Greenfield, Howie, 38
Guitar: electric, 3; "twangy," 45-
   46
Guthrie, Woody, 78

H-I

Haley, Bill, 10-11

Hamburg, as home of music clubs,
   64-65
Hammond, John, Jr., 100
Hard Day's Night, A, 68
Harrison, George, 64, 67
Hawkins, Ronnie, 99
Hawks, The, 99
Hell's Angels, 73
Helm, Levon, 99
Hendrix, Jimi, 33, 87-88
High Numbers, 92
Hillman, Chris, 82
Holland, Brian, 53
Holland, Eddie, 53
Holly, Buddy, 34-35
Howlin' Wolf, 7-8
Hudson, Garth, 99

Ink Spots, 16

J-K

Jackson Five, 57
Jackson, Michael, 57
Jagger, Mick, 70, 71, 73
Jardine, Al, 47
Jefferson Airplane, 83-85
Johnson, Robert, 7
Jones, Brian, 70, 72-73
Joplin, Janis, 87
Joplin, Scott, 4
Jordan, Louis, 6

Kantner, Paul, 84, 85
Kaufman, Murray, 15
Kaukonen, Jorma, 84, 85
King, Carole, 38
King, Riley "B. B.," 8-9
Kirshner, Don, 38
Knight, Gladys, 56

L

Lambert, Kit, 92, 93-94

Last Waltz, The, 101
Lennon, John, 64, 66, 68, 69
Lewis, Jerry Lee, 22-23
Lieber, Jerry, 39
Little Richard, 30-33, 67
Love, Darlene, 40
Love, Mike, 47
Lovin' Spoonful, 81

M

Mamas and the Papas, The, 82
Mann, Barry, 38-39
Manuel, Richard, 99
Manzarek, Ray, 96
Martha and the Vandellas, 55
Martin, George, 66
McCartney, Paul, 64, 66, 68, 69
McGuinn, Jim (Roger), 82
McPhatter, Clyde, 17
Mills Brothers, The, 16
Miracles, The, 52, 54
Monterey Pop Festival, 87, 95
Moon, Keith, 92, 93
Moore, Scotty, 28
Morganfeld, McKinely. *See* Muddy
   Waters
Morris, Steveland. *See* Wonder,
   Stevie
Morrison, Jim, 96, 97, 98, 99
Morrow, Bruce. *See* Cousin Brucey
Morton, Ferdinand "Jelly Roll," 4
Motown Records, 51-57
Motown sound, 49, 51-52, 53
Muddy Waters, 6-7
Multi-tracking, 40
Murry the K, 15
Music from Big Pink, 99

N-O

Nelson, Ricky, 44

Nevins, Al, 37-38

Oldham, Andrew Loog, 71
Ono, Yoko, 69
Orioles, The, 16
Overtracking. *See* Multi-tracking

P-Q

Parker, Colonel Tom, 29
Penniman, Richard. *See* Little
   Richard
Perkins, Carl, 22
Peter, Paul, and Mary, 78
Phillips, John, 82
Phillips, Michelle, 82
Phillips, Sam, 27-28, 29
Platters, The, 18
Polyrhythm, 58
Presley, Elvis Aaron, 26-30
Psychedelic rock, 72

R

Radio, transistor, 15
Reeves, Martha, 55
Rhythm and blues, 13-15, 71
Richards, Keith, 70, 71, 73
Robertson, (Jaime) Robbie, 99
Robinson, Smokey, 52, 54
Rockabilly, 21-22
Rodgers, Jimmie, 9
Rolling Stones, The, 70-74
Ronettes, The, 40
Ross, Diana, 55, 56

S

San Francisco Sound, 83-88
Santana, 86
Santana, Carlos, 86

Sebastian, John, 81
Sedaka, Neil, 38
Sergeant Pepper's Lonely Hearts Club Band, 68-69
Sheridan, Tony, 65
Simon and Garfunkel, 80-81
Simon, Paul, 80-81
Skiffle, 63-64
Slick, Grace, 84
Smith, Bob. *See* Wolfman Jack
Soft Parade, The, 98
Some Girls, 73
Soul music, 50, 57-60
Spector, Phil, 39-41
Spector, Ronnie, 40
Starkey, Richard. *See* Starr, Ringo
Starr, Ringo, 66
Stoller, Mike, 39
Street corner groups, 15-18
String band, 1-2
Stubbs, Levi, 53-54
Sun Records, 27-28
Supremes, The, 55-56
Surf music, 46
Surrealistic Pillow, 84
Sutcliffe, Stu, 64, 66
Swing, 5
Syncopation, 2, 4

T

Tammie Records, 52
Temptations, The, 54

Terrell, Tammie, 56
Their Satanic Majesties Request, 72
Tommy, 94, 95
Townsend, Pete, 92, 93, 94, 95
Turner, Tina, 59-60
Twist, the, 45

U-V-W-X-Y-Z

Ventures, 46
Volunteers, 84

Walker, Aaron "T-Bone," 4
Wall of sound, 40
Watts, Charlie, 70
Weil, Cynthia, 38-39
Western swing, 9-10
Who Sell Out, The, 94
Who, The, 91-95
Williams, King Hiram "Hank," 10
Wills, Bob, 9-10
Wilson, Brian, 47-48
Wilson, Carl, 47
Wilson, Dennis, 47, 48
Wilson, Jackie, 52
Wolfman Jack, 15
Wonder, Stevie, 56-57
Wood, Ron, 73
Woodstock, 103-104
Workingman's Dead, 86
Wyman, Bill, 70

Zimmerman, Robert. *See* Dylan, Bob